H

MICHIGAN

TRAVEL GUIDE

Larry J. Wagenaar
Izzi Bendall

AN OFFICIAL PUBLICATION OF THE

SPONSORED BY

Rollin M. Gerstacker Foundation

The Historical Society of Michigan
Lansing

Printed in the United States of America.

Exterior art by Kelly Hansen, Scooter Creative

On the cover:
o   In Cassopolis, the mural "Sanctuary and Deliverance" depicts the 1847 Kentucky Raid. Photo by Gene Kaiser/*South Bend Tribune*.
o   Children examine fossils at the Lakeshore Museum Center in Muskegon.
o   Built in the early 20th century, Crisp Point Lighthouse stands along the coast of Lake Superior.
o   The Monarch Butterfly Celebration is an annual event at the Ziibiwing Center of Anishinabe Culture & Lifeways in Mount Pleasant.
o   This 1956 Buick Centurion is among the vehicles on display at the Alfred P. Sloan Museum in Flint.
o   "Big John" welcomes visitors to the Iron Mountain Iron Mine in Vulcan.
o   The Castle Museum of Saginaw County History is housed in Saginaw's original post office.

CONTENTS

No. 10 Schoolhouse in Grandville's Heritage Park

Wigwam at Chippewa Nature Center in Midland

The Old Mill Museum in Dundee

Bay View Historical Museum in Petoskey

DeTour Reef Light (Photo by David Bardsley)

INTRODUCTION

When it comes to Michigan's history, there is truly something for everyone. Interested in the state's automotive heritage? Head over to the Ford Piquette Avenue Plant in Detroit. Like military history? Check out the USS *Silversides* Submarine Museum in Muskegon. If lighthouses pique your interest, why not visit the Point Iroquois Light Station in the Upper Peninsula?

Michigan is a state with rich cultural and heritage resources. And with so many history museums and historic sites—475 of which are included in this guide—there's always something new to see, learn, or experience in regards to our state's colorful history.

To assemble this guide, we sent out inclusion forms to history organizations throughout the state and inquired about their physical location(s). If an organization did not respond with updated material, we added the note "Information may not be current" to the end of its listing. This does not mean that the description is incorrect; it means that the information was secured prior to 2013. In any event, prices and hours inevitably change. Considering this, we recommend contacting the sites ahead of your visit to avoid any unpleasant surprises.

Please note that each of the following destinations is operated by a member organization of the Historical Society of Michigan, which is a requirement to be included in this publication. If your local institution or one you visit is not included, it likely means it is not an HSM member or we are unaware of it.

As a 501(c)(3) nonprofit educational organization, we rely partly on our members to support our programming, which includes the publication of this guide. To learn more about membership in our Society, turn to the final pages of this book or visit *www.hsmichigan.org/join*.

We hope that you find this book helpful as you explore all the Great Lakes State has to offer. After all, a walk through Michigan's history will lead you to some of its most interesting places.

ACKNOWLEDGMENTS

The sixth edition of the *Historic Michigan Travel Guide* could not have come together without the help of our sponsors, staff members, and board of trustees. Likewise, we are incredibly grateful for the hundreds of organizations that submitted information to the Historical Society of Michigan for inclusion.

I would like to thank my co-editor, Izzi Bendall, for all the hard work and many hours she put into developing this guide, which serves to promote cultural and heritage tourism in Michigan. We built on the work of the past two editions to create this new volume, which includes more than 50 percent more listings than the last.

I would also like to thank our major sponsors—Meijer, Consumers Energy, and the Rollin M. Gerstacker Foundation. Their help was critical in bringing this publication together, making it possible to do the extensive work of collecting the necessary data, revising our database systems, writing, editing, typesetting, and publishing. In addition, Meijer has provided distribution in all of its Michigan stores to make this new edition of the *Historic Michigan Travel Guide* widely available.

We would also like to thank Patricia Majher and Ann Weller for copyediting this publication, Jacob Makowski for his help in research and data entry, and Lucy Wagenaar for fact checking.

Larry J. Wagenaar
Executive Director, Historical Society of Michigan
Publisher, *Michigan History* Magazine

ABOUT THE LISTINGS

Requirements
To be included in the *Historic Michigan Travel Guide*, a history destination must have an exhibit or a visitor experience that is open to the public. The site must also be operated by an organizational member of the Historical Society of Michigan.

Organization
This book is divided by regions, which are defined in the map below. Within each section, sites are listed by cities and towns, which are arranged alphabetically. You may also search for organizations and cities using the index starting on page 167.

WESTERN

CENTRAL

EASTERN

NORTHERN

UPPER PENINSULA

Information
The following information, in whole or in part, is provided for each site:

- Name of the historic destination
- Physical location of the site followed by its GPS coordinates in decimal format
- Contact information including telephone, e-mail, and website
- Public hours
- Admission fee
- Site information including parking, wheelchair accessibility, and tour guide availability
- Description of the site and its attractions

WESTERN

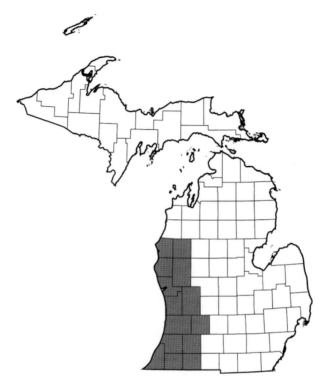

ADA

Averill Historical Museum of Ada
7144 Headley St., Ada, MI 49031 (42.956736, -85.491904)
(616) 676-9346, adahistoricalsociety@gmail.com,
www.adahistoricalsociety.org
Hours: Fri-Sat 1-4pm. Also by appointment. *Admission:* Donations
accepted. *Site Info:* On-site parking. Wheelchair accessible. Tour
guide available.

The Averill Historical Museum features a pantry, bedroom, and
parlor from an early 20th-century farmhouse. Exhibits pertain to
Ada's participation in WWI and WWII, the railroad in Ada, early
20th-century children's toys, early schools in Ada, Rix Robinson,
and Native Americans of the region. A temporary exhibit space
features something new twice a year. Adjacent to the museum is a
barn with several exhibits and a historical garden.

ALLEGAN

John C. Pahl Historic Village
150 Allegan County Fair Drive, Allegan, MI 49010 (42.536259, -85.859929)
(269) 673-8292, oldjailmuseum06@yahoo.com, www.alleganoldjail.org
Hours: Open during the Allegan County Fair and Allegan County Fiber Fest. *Site Info:* Wheelchair accessible. Special tours can be arranged with advance notice.

The John C. Pahl Historic Village is home to several buildings that have been moved to the Allegan County Fair Grounds. This includes a fire barn with a 1929 REO Fire Truck, a train depot building and C&O caboose, a house from the 1840s, and more.

Old Jail Museum
113 Walnut St., Allegan, MI 49010 (42.528341, -85.852894)
(269) 673-8292, oldjailmuseum06@yahoo.com, www.alleganoldjail.org
Hours: May-Aug: Fri-Sat 10am-4pm; Sep-Apr: Sat 10am-4pm. Also by appointment. *Admission:* Donations accepted. *Site Info:* Free street parking. Not wheelchair accessible. Guided tours available; advance notice required for large groups.

Built in 1906, the Allegan County Jail was converted into a museum in 1963. Today, the Old Jail Museum includes period rooms and displays. Exhibits contain items from the pioneer days up to 1950 and include artifacts from the War of 1812, Civil War, Spanish-American War, World War I, and World War II. The museum is accredited by the American Alliance of Museums and is listed in the National Register of Historic Places.

ALTO

Bowne Center School House
Southeast Corner of 84th Avenue and Alden Nash Road, Alto, MI 49302 (42.812316, -85.368871)
(616) 868-6424, srjohnson4@charter.net, www.bownehistory.org
Hours: Jun-Sep: 1st Sun monthly 2-4pm. Also by appointment. *Admission:* Donations accepted. *Site Info:* Free on-site parking. Partially wheelchair accessible. Self-guided.

The Bowne Center School House is filled with old desks, books, and other school artifacts.

Bowne Township Historical Museum
8240 Alden Nash Ave., Alto, MI 49302 (42.812861, -85.369354)
(616) 868-6424, srjohnson4@charter.net, www.bownehistory.org

Hours: Jun-Sep: 1st Sun monthly 2-4pm. Also by appointment.
Admission: Donations accepted. *Site Info:* Free on-site parking.
Partially wheelchair accessible. Self-guided.

The Bowne Township Historical Museum is home to many items
related to the history of Bowne Center and Bowne Township.

BALDWIN

Shrine of the Pines
8962 S. M-37, Baldwin, MI 49304 (43.971816, -85.841588)
(231) 745-7892, www.facebook.com/shrineofthepines
Hours: Mid-May to mid-Oct: Mon-Sat 10am-6pm, Sun 1:30-6pm.
Last daily tour at 5:30pm. *Admission:* Adults $5, Seniors $4, Youth
(6-17) $2.50, Family $12.50, and Children (0-5) free.

The Shrine of the Pines is located in a hunting lodge that displays
furniture made from pine stumps by Raymond W. Overholzer.
Overholzer fashioned beds, chairs, chandeliers, etc.—without using
metal fasteners or varnish. One highlight is a dining room table
made from a 700-pound stump.

BENTON HARBOR

Mary's City of David
1158 E. Britain Ave., Benton Harbor, MI 49023 (42.10853,
-86.43034)
(269) 925-1601, rjtaylor@maryscityofdavid.org,
www.maryscityofdavid.org
Hours: Sat-Sun 1-5pm. *Admission:* $1. *Site Info:* Free on-site
parking. Wheelchair accessible. Tour guide available Jun-Sep;
$4/person.

Mary's City of David has a history that spans 110 years in
Michigan. Today, the organization hosts a museum and tours on its
property, which is listed in the National Register of Historic Places.
The site includes 81 structures, 11 of which are available for
viewing. The museum, which tells the story of the Israelite House of
David and its reorganization of 1930, is located in Mary's
Auditorium.

BERRIEN SPRINGS

History Center at Courthouse Square
313 N. Cass St., Berrien Springs, MI 49103 (41.947892,
-86.340753)
(269) 471-1202, kcyr@berrienhistory.org, www.berrienhistory.org
Hours: Sep-May: Mon-Fri 10am-5pm; Jun-Aug: Mon-Sat 10am-

5pm. *Admission:* Free. *Site Info:* Free on-site parking. Partially wheelchair accessible. Tour guide available by appointment.

The Berrien County Historical Association operates the History Center at Courthouse Square, which includes the oldest complex of county government buildings in the Midwest. This complex includes a 1839 courthouse, 1830 log house, 1870 sheriff's residence, and 1860/1873 office building. The museum features permanent and special exhibits highlighting regional history.

BRETHREN

Brethren Heritage Association
Corner of Cart Avenue & Amick Street, Brethren, MI 49619 (44.306184, -86.015208)
(231) 477-5526, janetdonstroup@gmail.com
Hours: Summer: Sun 1-4pm. Also by appointment; call (231) 477-5525 or (231) 477-5539. *Admission:* Donations accepted. *Site Info:* Street parking. Wheelchair accessible. Tour guide available by appointment.

The Brethren Heritage Association preserves the heritage of the area's lumbering/farming community that originated in the early 1900s. The association maintains its museum in a former store and ice house. On display are models of all of the township's one-room schools as well as a scale model of the nationally renowned High Bridge, a 96-foot-high railroad bridge that once crossed the Big Manistee River. (The original bridge was torn down in 1955.)

BYRON CENTER

Byron Center Museum and Historical Society
2506 Prescott Ave. SW, Byron Center, MI 49315 (42.810979, -85.725624)
(616) 878-0888, susan@byroncenterhistory.org,
www.commoncorners.com/kent/kent_byron_bchs.htm
Hours: Call for hours. *Admission:* Free. *Site Info:* Free on-site parking. Wheelchair accessible. Tour guide available by appointment.

Located in the 1876 town hall, the Byron Area Historical Museum features multiple exhibits, including a country store, doctor's office, schoolhouse, military room, parlor/dining room, farming area, etc.

CALEDONIA

Caledonia Historical Museum
8196 Broadmoor Ave. SE, Caledonia, MI 49316 (42.815543, -85.509274)

(616) 260-0052, gackler@iserv.net,
www.angelfire.com/mi/CaledoniaHistory
Hours: By appointment. *Admission:* Free. *Site Info:* On-site parking.
Wheelchair accessible. Tour guide available by appointment.

Located in the Caledonia Township Hall, the Caledonia Historical
Museum has a limited collection available for public viewing.

CANNONSBURG

Cannon Township Historical Museum

8045 Cannonsburg Road, Cannonsburg, MI 49317 (43.054264,
-85.469133)
(616) 874-6865
Hours: May-Sep: Sun 2-4pm. Also by appointment. *Admission:*
Free. *Site Info:* Free nearby parking. Wheelchair accessible. Self-
guided.

The Cannon Township Historical Society preserves its history in the
former township hall.

CASSOPOLIS

Edward Lowe Information and Legacy Center

58220 Decatur Road, Cassopolis, MI 49031 (41.954112,
-85.973038)
(269) 445-4200, heidi@lowe.org, www.edwardlowe.org
Hours: Mon-Fri 8am-5pm. *Admission:* Free. *Site Info:* Free on-site
parking. Wheelchair accessible. Self-guided. Tours held Wed at 2pm
(Apr-Oct); call for reservations.

The Edward Lowe Foundation was founded by Edward Lowe, who
invented Kitty Litter in 1947. Today, the organization's information
center features an exhibit about Lowe's business ventures and the
foundation. This includes videos, print materials, a live web feed,
and photos and artifacts dating back to the 1940s.

Red Brick Schoolhouse Museum

63600 Brick Church St., Cassopolis, MI 49031 (41.874298,
-86.010018)
*(269) 445-4456, wuepperj@gmail.com,
www.casscountymi.org/HistoricalCommission.aspx*
Hours: By appointment. *Site Info:* On-site parking.

Administered by the Cass County Historical Commission, the Red
Brick Schoolhouse Museum presents a one-room, rural school
complete with books, furniture, and maps.
* Information may not be current.

CENTREVILLE

Centreville Museum & History Library
113 E. Main St. Centreville, MI 49032 (41.923689, -85.526491)
(269) 483-7122, mstarmann@yahoo.com,
www.hstarmann.wix.com/sjchs
Hours: By appointment. *Admission:* Donations accepted. *Site Info:*
Free street and on-site parking. Wheelchair accessible. Tour guide
available by appointment.

The Centreville Museum & History Library is located in the former
Klesner Hotel, which was built circa 1860 and is now listed in the
State Register of Historic Sites. The building is currently being
restored by the St. Joseph County Historical Society and serves as
the organization's main headquarters and library.

CHASE

Chase Township Public Library
8400 E. North St., Chase, MI 49623 (43.889634, -85.634198)
(231) 832-9511, chaselibrary@yahoo.com
Hours: Mon 10am-6pm, Tue 9am-5pm, Wed-Thu 10am-6pm. Also
open Sat 9am-12pm during the school year. *Admission:* Free. *Site
Info:* Wheelchair accessible.

The Chase Library Historical Society records and researches local
history and families, with a focus on Chase, Pinora, Cherry Valley,
and Yates townships. The society maintains changing displays at the
Chase Township Public Library.

COLOMA

North Berrien Historical Museum
300 Coloma Ave., Coloma, MI 49038 (42.181565, -86.312561)
(269) 468-3330, info@northberrienhistory.org,
www.northberrienhistory.org
Hours: Summer: Tue-Sat 10am-4pm; Winter:Tue-Fri 10am-4pm.
Admission: Free. *Site Info:* Free on-site parking. Wheelchair
accessible. Self-guided.

The North Berrien Historical Museum focuses on the local history
of northern Berrien County. The main gallery features the history of
Native Americans, lake resorts, rural schools, Lake Michigan
shipwrecks, daily life, and businesses including the Watervliet Paper
Mill. The Nichols Agricultural Building holds farm equipment,
lumbering tools, and transportation displays. Highlights include a
1934 Parrett Tractor and a fruit grading machine, both used by local
fruit farmers.

COLON

Community Historical Museum of Colon
Farrand-Hoekzema Annex

219 N. Blackstone Ave., Colon, MI 49040 (41.960190, -85.325084)
(269) 432-3804, www.colonmi.com/historical.html
Hours: Jun-Aug: Tue and Thu 2-4:30pm. Also by appointment.
Admission: Donations accepted. *Site Info:* Parking at the Methodist
church. Wheelchair accessible. Tour guide available; donations
accepted.

As Colon refers to itself as the "Magic Capital of the World," the
Colon Community Historical Museum houses a magic collection. It
also has a print shop and displays area artifacts pertaining to
medicine, school, Native Americans, pioneers, general store, toys,
military, and more. Also on site is the Farrand-Hoekzema Annex,
which includes a woolen mill, kitchen, parlor, bedroom, doctor's
office, and schoolroom.

COMSTOCK PARK

Alpine Township Historical Museum

2408 Seven Mile Road NW, Comstock Park, MI 49321 (43.058827,
-85.690219)
(616) 784-1262, b.alt@alpinetwp.org, www.alpinetwp.org
Hours: By appointment. *Admission:* Free. *Site Info:* Public parking.
Wheelchair accessible. Tour guide available.

Maintained by the Alpine Township Historical Commission, the
Alpine Township Historical Museum is located in the 1860
township hall. It is listed in the State Register of Historic Sites.

COOPERSVILLE

Coopersville Area Historical Society Museum

363 Main St., Coopersville, MI 49404 (43.065862, -85.936147)
(616) 997-7240, historicalsoc@allcom.net,
www.coopersvillehistoricalmuseum.org
Hours: Tue 3-7pm, Wed 10am-1pm, Fri 1-5pm, Sat 10am-4pm.
Also by appointment. *Admission:* Donations accepted. *Site Info:*
Free street and on-site parking. Wheelchair accessible. Call ahead
for tour guide availability.

Located in a former interurban railroad depot and substation, the
Coopersville Area Historical Society Museum is listed in the State
Register of Historic Sites and National Register of Historic Places.
The gold records, photographs, and memorabilia of early rock 'n'
roll star Del Shannon are a major attraction. A connecting building
houses a full-size sawmill, model logging railroad, and early

schoolroom. Also on the grounds is "Merlin," a rare interurban passenger car.

Coopersville Farm Museum & Event Center

375 Main St., Coopersville, MI 49404 (43.064529, -85.936861)
(616) 997-8555, info@coopersvillefarmmuseum.org,
www.coopersvillefarmmuseum.org
Hours: Jul-Oct: Tue-Sat 10am-4pm; Nov-Jun: Tue, Thu, Sat 10am-2pm. *Admission:* Adults $4, Youth $2, Children (0-3) free. *Site Info:* Wheelchair accessible. Free on-site parking.

The Coopersville Farm Museum & Event Center honors farming, agriculture, and rural life through art, exhibits, and events. The museum also features interactive exhibits and a children's area.

DECATUR

Newton House

20689 Marcellus Hwy., Decatur, MI 49045 (42.012379, -85.967373)
(269) 445-4456, wuepperj@gmail.com,
www.casscountymi.org/HistoricalCommission.aspx
Hours: May-Oct: 1st Sun monthly 1-4:30pm. Also by appointment.
Site Info: On-site parking.

This restored, mid-19th-century Quaker home is owned by Michigan State University and maintained by the Cass County Historical Commission.
* Information may not be current.

DOUGLAS

History Center (The Old School House)

130 Center St., Douglas, MI 49406 (42.643712, -86.203868)
(269) 857-5751, fnschmidt@wmol.com, www.sdhistoricalsociety.org
Hours: Varies by season. See website. *Admission:* Donations accepted. *Site Info:* On-site and street parking. Wheelchair accessible. E-mail for tour information.

The 1866 Old School House, or the Douglas Union School, is the oldest multi-classroom school building in Michigan. Today, it is used as a history center, and its attractions include a lifeboat exhibit, back-in-time garden, history room, and more.

DOWAGIAC

Dowagiac Area History Museum

201 E. Division St., Dowagiac, MI 49047 (41.984237, -86.105732)
(269) 783-2560, sarseneau@dowagiac.org,
www.facebook.com/DowagiacAreaHistoryMuseum

Hours: Tue-Fri 10am-5pm, Sat 11am-3pm. *Admission:* Free. *Site Info:* Free street and on-site parking. Wheelchair accessible. Self-guided.

The newly renovated Dowagiac Area History Museum examines the history of Dowagiac, Cass County, and Sister Lakes. Exhibits include "Industrial Dowagiac," a model train set of 1920 Dowagiac, the Round Oak Stove Company, Heddon Bait Company, the Underground Railroad, Potawatomi Indians, and early settlement.

Heddon Museum
414 West St., Dowagiac, MI 49047 (41.986853, -86.116327)
(269) 782-4068, heddonmuseum@lyonsindustries.com,
www.heddonmuseum.org
Hours: Tue 6:30-8:30pm, Last Sun monthly 1:30-4pm. Also by appointment; call Don or Joan at (269) 782-5698. *Admission:* Donations accepted. *Site Info:* Free street and on-site parking. Wheelchair accessible. Tour guide available; donations accepted from large groups.

Located in the former Heddon factory, the Heddon Museum preserves the history of the James Heddon family. At one time, the James Heddon's Sons Co. was the world's largest fishing tackle manufacturer. On display are more than 1,000 Heddon lures, 140 reels, and 150 Heddon rods, including an original James Heddon frog, one of the most sought-after collector lures. Other highlights include the Heddon truck, a boat, and car-related memorabilia.

EDWARDSBURG

Edwardsburg Area Historical Museum
28616 Main St., Edwardsburg, MI 49112 (41.798355, -86.084656)
joboepple@aol.com, Find on Facebook
Hours: Mon-Sat 1-4pm. *Admission:* $2 donation. *Site Info:* Free street parking. Wheelchair accessible. Tour guide available.

The Edwardsburg Historical Collection shares its community's history from the 1800s through today.

GALESBURG

Galesburg Historical Museum
190 E. Michigan Ave., Galesburg, MI 49053 (42.288693, -85.413296)
(269) 665-9011, www.galesburgmi.com
Hours: Wed 4:30-6pm, Sat 10am-2pm. *Admission:* Donations accepted. *Site Info:* On-site parking. Wheelchair accessible. Tour guide available by appointment; call Keith Martin at (269) 665-9953.

The Galesburg Historical Museum serves as a repository for artifacts from the Galesburg and surrounding area. The museum's exhibits include an 1860s linear four-room house with a kitchen, parlor, dining room, and bedroom.

GRAND HAVEN

Grand Trunk Depot Museum of Transportation
1 N. Harbor Drive, Grand Haven, MI 49417 (43.064921, -86.2340871)
(616) 842-0700, kpott@tri-citiesmuseum.org, www.tri-citiesmuseum.org
Hours: Summer: Tue-Fri 10am-8pm, Sat-Sun 12-8pm. *Admission:* Donations accepted. *Site Info:* Free street and on-site parking. Wheelchair accessible.

The Grand Trunk Depot Museum of Transportation is located in the restored 1870 Detroit & Milwaukee Depot and showcases the history of railroading, automobiles, and maritime history on the Great Lakes.

Tri-Cities Historical Museum
200 Washington Ave., Grand Haven, MI 49417 (43.063632, -86.230905)
(616) 842-0700, kpott@tri-citiesmuseum.org, www.tri-citiesmuseum.org
Hours: Summer: Tue-Fri 10am-8pm, Sat-Sun 12-8pm. Winter: Tue-Fri 10am-5pm, Sat-Sun 12-5pm. *Admission:* Donations accepted. *Site Info:* Free street and on-site parking. Wheelchair accessible. Self-guided.

Located in the newly renovated Akeley Building, the Tri-Cities Historical Museum details the development and history of Northwest Ottawa County. Exhibits include an authentic Native American wickiup, the 1920s Ekkens Store, and a recreated Bastian and Blessing soda fountain. Displays relate to local/state geology, fur trading, lumbering, pioneers, farming, industry, banking, business, building, and general living.

GRAND RAPIDS

Cascade Historical Society Museum
2839 Thornapple River Drive, Grand Rapids, MI 49546 (42.912632, -85.497488)
(616) 868-6465, vicsugoblu@comcast.net, www.cascadetwp.com
Hours: By appointment. *Admission:* Free. *Site Info:* Free street parking. Wheelchair accessible. Tour guide available.

The Cascade Historical Society Museum is located in the former township hall, which was built in the 19th century. Today, it features artifacts, photographs, and limited exhibits.

Gerald R. Ford Presidential Museum

303 Pearl St. NW, Grand Rapids, MI 49504 (42.968215, -85.677427)
(616) 254-0400, ford.museum@nara.gov,
www.fordlibrarymuseum.gov
Hours: Daily 9am-5pm. *Admission:* Adults $7, Seniors $6, Youth $3, Children (0-5) free. *Site Info:* Free on-site parking. Wheelchair accessible.

Part of the Presidential Libraries system of the National Archives and Records Administration, the Gerald R. Ford Presidential Museum is located in the hometown and congressional district of former President Ford. The museum provides extensive exhibits on the life and career of the 38th president of the United States.

Grand Rapids Public Museum

272 Pearl St. NW, Grand Rapids, MI 49504 (42.965707, -85.676671)
(616) 929-1700, info@grmuseum.org, www.grmuseum.org
Hours: Mon-Sat 9am-5pm, Sun 12-5pm. Closed Easter, Thanksgiving, Christmas, and New Year's Day. *Admission:* Adults $8, Seniors (62+) $7, Youth (3-17) $3, Children (0-2) free. Additional charges for special shows and exhibits. *Site Info:* Parking ramp across the street. Wheelchair accessible.

Founded in 1854, the Grand Rapids Public Museum is Michigan's oldest and third largest museum. The facility collects, preserves, and presents the natural, cultural, and social history of the region. Permanent exhibits include a full-scale recreation of Grand Rapids in the 1890s, a complete history of furniture manufacturing in West Michigan, more than 600 artifacts and images depicting diversity in West Michigan, and more.

Heritage Hill Historic District

126 College Ave. SE, Grand Rapids, MI 49503 (42.960368, -85.656564)
(616) 459-8950, heritage@heritagehillweb.org,
www.heritagehillweb.org

The Heritage Hill Association offers a self-guided walking tour of Heritage Hill Historic District, the oldest neighborhood in Grand Rapids. Available for download on the association's website, the tour brochure highlights examples of most American architectural styles from the 19th and 20th centuries.

Michigan Masonic Museum & Library

233 E. Fulton St., Ste. 10, Grand Rapids, MI 49503 (42.963395, -85.662439)
(616) 459-9336, booktinker@yahoo.com; library@mi-gl.org, www.masonichistory.org
Hours: Mon-Fri 10am-6pm. Every other Sat 10am-3pm. *Admission:* Free. *Site Info:* Free parking in the adjoining ramp. Wheelchair accessible. Tour guide available by appointment.

Housed in the lower level of the historic Grand Rapids Masonic Center, the Michigan Masonic Museum & Library is dedicated to educating the public about Free Masonry. The museum is home to a wealth of Masonic memorabilia, such as Masonic aprons dating from the 1700s, swords and other ceremonial gear, officer jewels dating from the mid-1850s, and an array of uniforms and costumes.

Temple Emanuel of Grand Rapids Archives

1715 E. Fulton, Grand Rapids, MI 49506 (42.963398, -85.626969)
(616) 459-5976, www.templeemanuelgr.org
Hours: By appointment. *Admission:* Free. *Site Info:* Wheelchair accessible. Parking behind building. Tour guide available; call ahead.

The Temple Emanuel of Grand Rapids Archives keeps and preserves important documents pertaining to the temple's activities and history. Display cases contain important documents, including a 350-year-old Torah that the Nazis confiscated from Czechoslovakia, a letter from Rabbi Isaac Mayer Wise, etc. Built in 1952-1953, the current temple was designed by Eric Mendelsohn and features Tiffany windows from the original 1881 building.

Voigt House Victorian Museum

115 College Ave. SE, Grand Rapids, MI 49503 (42.960645, -85.657458)
(616) 929-1749, *info@grmuseum.org, www.grmuseum.org*
Site Info: Not wheelchair accessible.

Located in historic Heritage Hill, the Voigt House Victorian Museum was once the home of the well-known Voigt family, who were successful merchants and flour-mill entrepreneurs in the Grand Rapids area. Completed in 1896, the three-story brick mansion is now a property of the Grand Rapids Public Museum.

GRANDVILLE

Grandville Museum

3195 Wilson Ave. SW, Grandville, MI 49418 (42.906964, -85.763544)
(616) 531-3030, grandvilleHC@hotmail.com

Hours: 1st Thu monthly 1-4pm. 2nd Mon monthly in the evening. Also by appointment. *Admission:* Free. *Site Info:* Free on-site parking. Wheelchair accessible. Tour guide available during open hours and by appointment.

Located on the lower level of Grandville City Hall, the Grandville Museum features several items that were donated by area residents.

No. 10 Schoolhouse

Heritage Park on Canal Avenue (near 44th Street), Grandville, MI 49418 (42.886856, -85.770517)
(616) 531-3030, grandvilleHC@hotmail.com
Hours: By appointment. *Admission:* Free. *Site Info:* Free on-site parking. Wheelchair accessible. Tour guide available during open hours and by appointment.

The No. 10 Schoolhouse has original desks, pictures of students, old books, chalk boards, clothing to try on, teacher quarters, and bell.

HART

Hart Historic District

570 E. Lincoln, Hart, MI 49420 (43.700523, -86.3583783)
(231) 873-2488, ggoldberg@ci.hart.mi.us, www.ci.hart.mi.us
Hours: Jun-Sep: Tue-Sat 11am-4pm. Also by appointment. *Admission:* Self-guided Tour $5, Guided Tour $8. *Site Info:* Free on-site parking. Partially wheelchair accessible. Tour guide available; refer to admission for pricing.

Managed jointly by the Heritage Preservation Group and the Hart Historic Commission, the downtown Hart Historic District includes several buildings of historical significance: an 1858 Native American log cabin, the 1868 Hart railroad depot, the 1897 Sackrider Church, and more. Displays within these buildings feature everything from WWII memorabilia to a miniature piano collection.

HARTFORD

Van Buren County Historical Museum

58471 Red Arrow Hwy., Hartford, MI 49057 (42.213937, -86.112599)
(269) 621-2188
Hours: Jun-Sep: Wed and Fri-Sat 12-5pm. *Admission:* Adults $5, Children (0-12) $1. *Site Info:* On-site parking. Wheelchair accessible. Tour guide available; private tours by appointment.

Located in the former county poorhouse, the Van Buren County Historical Museum features three floors of historical items and exhibits. This includes a one-room school, general store, music room, old-fashioned kitchen, turn-of-the-century parlor, dentist office, and military room. There is also a replica log cabin and blacksmith works on the grounds.

HASTINGS

Historic Charlton Park Village, Museum & Recreation Area
2545 S. Charlton Park Road, Hastings, MI 49058 (42.617830, -85.207729)
(269) 945-3775, info@charltonpark.org, www.charltonpark.org
Hours: Daily 9am-4pm. Closed in winter. *Admission:* Free, except during special events. *Site Info:* Free on-site parking except during special events. Partially wheelchair accessible. Tour guide available by appointment; call Shannon Ritzer at (269) 945-3775. Cost is $5/person.

Representing a typical mid-Michigan village of the late 1800s to early 1900s, Historic Charlton Park features 25 buildings that include a blacksmith shop, township hall, hardware store, and more. Brochures for the walking tour are available by the village signpost near the Wm. A. Upjohn House Visitor Center.

HICKORY CORNERS

Gilmore Car Museum
6865 Hickory Road, Hickory Corners, MI 49060 (42.442136, -85.422932)
(616) 671-5089, info@gilmorecarmuseum.org, www.gilmorecarmuseum.org
Hours: Mon-Fri 9am-5pm, Sat-Sun 9am-6pm. *Admission:* Adults $12, Seniors $11, Youth $9, Children (0-6) free. School tours are free. *Site Info:* Free on-site parking. Partially wheelchair accessible. Self-guided. See website for schedule of car shows.

The 90-acre Gilmore Car Museum campus is home to nearly 400 cars, trucks, and motorcycles. There are four recreated car dealerships, a 1930s gas station, and an authentic 1940s diner. On display are more than 1,600 hood ornaments, 100+ children's pedal cars, and the one-of-a-kind movie set and car from the 1967 Walt Disney movie "The Gnome-Mobile." The campus is also home to a collection of several independent museums, including the Classic Car Club of America Museum, Pierce-Arrow Museum, Model A Ford Museum, and others.

HOLLAND

Cappon House and Settlers House Museums
228 W. 9th St., Holland, MI 49424 (42.788998, -86.117444)
(616) 796-3329, hollandmuseum@hollandmuseum.org,

www.hollandmuseum.org
Hours: May-Dec: Fri-Sat 12-4pm. *Admission:* $5, Children (0-5) free. *Site Info:* Free street parking. Not wheelchair accessible. Tour guide available.

A visitor center in the Cappon barn is the starting point for touring the Cappon House and nearby Settlers House. The Italianate Cappon House was built by Holland's first mayor and tannery owner, Isaac Cappon, after the Holland Fire of 1871. The Settlers House was one of the few buildings to survive the fire in 1871 and recalls the hardships faced during the Holland area's settlement period.

Center of African American Art and History
21 W. 16th St., Holland, MI 49423 (42.783274, -86.108265)
(616) 836-8559, www.caaahholland.org
Hours: See website. *Admission:* Adults $8, Seniors (65+) $6, Youth (7-17) $6, Children (0-6) free.

The Center of African American Art and History collects, preserves, interprets, documents, and exhibits the rich contributions of African Americans from the state's earliest history to the present and future. **Information may not be current.*

The Felt Estate
6597 138th, Holland, MI 49423 (42.697040, -86.194009)
(616) 335-8982, events@feltmansion.org; www.feltmansion.org
Hours: See website. *Admission:* Adults $10, Seniors & Students $8. *Site Info:* Free on-site parking. Partially wheelchair accessible. Tour guide available by appointment.

In addition to serving as the home of the Felt family, the 1920s mansion also served as housing for the St. Augustine Seminary prep school and as office space when the state used the property for a prison. Today, the Felt Estate features a collection of Comptometers, a key-driven mechanical calculator that was invented by Dorr Felt.

Holland Armory
16 W. 9th St., Holland, MI 49423 (42.789358, -86.107895)
(616) 796-3329, hollandmuseum@hollandmuseum.org,
www.hollandmuseum.org
Admission: Free. *Hours:* By appointment. *Site Info:* Free street parking. Wheelchair accessible. Self-guided.

Housed in the Holland Armory are the administrative offices of the Holland Historical Trust and an interpretive exhibit about Holland's National Guard.

Holland Museum

31 W. 10th St., Holland, MI 49423 (42.788724, -86.108566)
(616) 796-3329, hollandmuseum@hollandmuseum.org,
www.hollandmuseum.org
Hours: May-Oct: Mon and Wed-Sat 10am-5pm, Sun 12-5pm.
Admission: Adults $7, Seniors $6, Students $4, Children (0-5) free.
Site Info: Free street parking. Wheelchair accessible. Tour guide
available.

Located in the 1914 post office, the Holland Museum houses
cultural attractions from the "old country," including Dutch
paintings/decorative arts and exhibits from the Netherlands Pavilion
of the 1939 New York World's Fair. The museum also features local
history, including Lake Michigan shipwrecks and resorts;
agriculture and manufacturing; religious foundations of the "Holland
Kolonie"; and an illustrated timeline of area history including its
increasing ethnic diversity.

Joint Archives of Holland

Theil Research Center, 9 E. 10th St., Holland, MI 49423
(42.788608, -86.106736)
(616) 395-7798, archives@hope.edu, www.jointarchives.org
Hours: Mon-Fri 8am-12pm and 1-5pm. *Admission:* Free. *Site Info:*
Free street parking. Wheelchair accessible. Tour guide available by
appointment.

A department of Hope College, the Joint Archives of Holland
promotes the educational mission of Hope College and its partner
institutions by actively collecting, caring for, interpreting, and
making available the unique historical resources in its care. An
abbreviated version of "Campus Alive: A Walking Tour of Hope
College" is available on the archives' website. Visitors may also
purchase the complete booklet from the archives for $1.95.

JENISON

Jenison Museum

28 Port Sheldon Road, Jenison, MI 49429 (42.886426, -85.824503)
(616) 457-4398, info@jenisonhistory.org, www.jenisonhistory.org
Hours: 1st Tue monthly 10am-12pm, 3rd Sat monthly 2pm-4pm.
Admission: Donations accepted. *Site Info:* Free on-site parking. Not
wheelchair accessible. Self-guided.

The Jenison Historical Association oversees and cares for this turn-
of-the-century house, which is decorated with period-appropriate
furnishings and features several displays regarding the history of the
Jenison area. This includes "Then and Now," which compares
Jenison of the past with its present, as well as a display about the
interurban railroad that once ran through Jenison.

KALAMAZOO

Kalamazoo Valley Museum
230 N. Rose St., Kalamazoo, MI 49007 (42.293389, -85.583742)
(269) 373-7990, www.kalamazoomuseum.org
Hours: Oct-May: Mon-Sat 9am-5pm, Sun & Holidays 1-5pm.
Closed Easter, Thanksgiving, Christmas Eve, and Christmas Day.
Admission: Free. *Site Info:* Metered street parking or parking ramp
($1.20/hour). Wheelchair accessible. Self-guided.

Kalamazoo Valley Museum features exhibits on science,
technology, and the history of Southwest Michigan. Attractions
include a planetarium, self-directed play area for children (ages 2-5),
and national traveling exhibits. History exhibits explore the products
that have made Kalamazoo famous and its growth from a frontier
town to a prosperous city. Visitors can also get a feel for the
community at the Douglass Community Center and WKVM TV-
station displays.

KENTWOOD

Heritage Room at the Richard L. Root Branch Library
4950 Breton Ave. SE, Kentwood, MI 49518 (42.874482,
-85.5968369)
(616) 554-0709, golderl@ci.kentwood.mi.us,
www.ci.kentwood.mi.us/committees/historical
Hours: Open during library's operating hours; refer to *www.kdl.org*.
Site Info: Free on-site parking. Wheelchair accessible. Self-guided.

The Heritage Room houses the artifacts, photographs, cemetery
records, and other historical documents entrusted to the Kentwood
Historic Preservation Commission. The commission sometimes
displays themed exhibits pertaining to the area's history from its
beginnings as Paris Township through today.

LOWELL

Lowell Area Historical Museum
325 W. Main St., Lowell, MI 49331 (42.933935, -85.341635)
(616) 897-7688, history@lowellmuseum.org,
www.lowellmuseum.org
Hours: Tue 1-4pm, Thu 1-8pm, Sat-Sun 1-4pm. *Admission:* Adults
$3, Children (5-17) $1.50, Children (0-4) free. *Site Info:* Free on-site
parking. Wheelchair accessible. Tour guide available.

The Lowell Area Historical Museum is housed in the Graham
Building, which was built in 1873 and used as a residential duplex.
Today, the building features Victorian rooms with exhibits about
early Lowell history, business and industry, and the Lowell

Showboat. It is listed in the National Register of Historic Places.

LUDINGTON

Big Sable Point Lighthouse
5611 N. Lighthouse Drive, Ludington, MI 49431 (44.057322, -86.513772)
(231) 845-7417, splkadirector@gmail.com, www.splka.org
Hours: Daily 10am-5pm. *Site Info:* Michigan Recreation Passport is required for entry; parking lot is 1.8 miles away from structure. Not wheelchair accessible. Self-guided.

Owned by Ludington State Park and operated by the Sable Points Lighthouse Keepers Association, Big Sable Point Lighthouse was built in 1867 and stands at 112 feet tall. Visitors can watch a history movie and those who pay a donation of $3/adult and $1/child can climb the 130 steps to the top of the tower. Visitors must be at least 36 inches tall to climb.

Ludington North Breakwater Light
107 S. Harrison St., Ludington, MI 49431 (43.954880, -86.446191)
(231) 845-7417, splkadirector@gmail.com, www.splka.org
Hours: Daily 10am-5pm. *Site Info:* Vehicles can park at the Stearns Park parking lot located just north of U.S. 10 off of Lakeshore Drive for no charge. Not wheelchair accessible. Self-guided.

Located down the shore from Big Sable, the Ludington North Breakwater Lighthouse was lit in 1924 and stands at 57 feet tall. With a donation of $3/adult and $1/child, a person can climb to the top of the tower. Visitors must be at least 36 inches tall to climb.

S.S. *Badger*
701 Maritime Drive, Ludington, MI 49431 (43.949197, -86.450123)
(231) 843-1509, tbrown@ssbadger.com, www.ssbadger.com
Hours: May 6-Oct 13. *Admission:* Travel fare prices listed on website. *Site Info:* On-site parking available for a fee. Wheelchair accessible. Self-guided.

The only coal-fired steamship still in operation in the United States, the S.S. *Badger* transports passengers and vehicles between Ludington, Michigan, and Manitowoc, Wisconsin. The ferry, which is listed in the National Register of Historic Places, has a room with displays detailing maritime history.

MEARS

Little Sable Point Lighthouse
287 N. Lighthouse Drive, Mears, MI 49436 (43.651354,

-86.539531)
(231) 845-7417, splkadirector@gmail.com, www.splka.org
Hours: Daily 10am-5pm. *Site Info:* Michigan Recreation Passport is required for entry. Not wheelchair accessible. Self-guided.

For a donation of $3/adult and $1/child, visitors can climb the 115-foot-tall tower of the Little Sable Point Lighthouse, which was completed in 1874. Visitors must be at least 36 inches tall to climb.

Oceana Historical Park & Museum
5783 Fox Road, Mears, MI 49436 (43.681940, -86.422383)
(231) 873-2600, www.oceanahistory.org
Hours: Jun-Aug: Sat-Sun 1-4pm. *Admission:* Free admission. *Site Info:* Free street and on-site parking. Wheelchair accessible. Tour guide available; special tours by appointment.

The Oceana Historical Park & Museum contains a transportation museum, the home of Swift Lathers (editor of *The Mears Newz*), a tool museum, an early mission church, an early 20th-century Lake Michigan cottage, a trapper's cabin, and the former Mears town hall. Special exhibits change annually.

MUSKEGON

Fire Barn Museum
510 W. Clay Ave., Muskegon, MI 49440 (43.232525, -86.255904)
(231) 722-0278, info@lakeshoremuseum.org,
www.lakeshoremuseum.org
Hours: May-Oct: Wed-Sun 12-4pm. Special holiday tours are offered between Thanksgiving and New Year's Day. *Admission:* Free. *Site Info:* Free street parking. Partially wheelchair accessible; first floor only. Self-guided.

The Fire Barn Museum is a replica of the Hackley Hose Company No. 2, which was formed in 1875 after the city experienced several devastating fires. Artifacts on display include a 1923 LaFrance Class B Pumper Truck, hose carts, hooks and ladders, alarm and call box systems, and photographs of local fires. The second floor features a uniform display and the living quarters of early firefighters.

Hackley and Hume Historic Site
484 W. Webster Ave., Muskegon, MI 49440 (43.231530, -86.255243)
(231) 722-0278, info@lakeshoremuseum.org,
www.lakeshoremuseum.org
Hours: May-Oct: Wed-Sun 12-4pm. Special holiday tours offered between Thanksgiving and New Year's Day. *Admission:* Adults (13+) $5, Children (0-12) free. Admission is free in October. *Site Info:* Free street and on-site parking. Not wheelchair accessible.

Tour guide available; appointment required for groups of 10 or more.

The restored homes of Muskegon's most famous lumber barons, Charles H. Hackley and Thomas Hume, are two of the finest examples of Queen Anne-style homes in the country. Built in the late 1800s, the buildings feature lavish woodcarvings, stenciling, stained-glass windows, and period furnishings. Tours of the homes last approximately 75 minutes.

Lakeshore Museum Center

430 W. Clay Ave., Muskegon, MI 49440 (43.233515, -86.254133)
(231) 722-0278, info@lakeshoremuseum.org,
www.lakeshoremuseum.org
Hours: Mon-Fri 9:30am-4:30pm, Sat-Sun 12-4pm. *Admission:* Free.
Site Info: Free street and on-site parking. Wheelchair accessible.
Self-guided.

The Lakeshore Museum Center preserves and interprets the natural and cultural history of Muskegon County through exhibits, education, and programs. The exhibit "Michigan Through the Depths of Time" takes visitors on a 400-million-year journey that begins under the sea and continues through the Ice Age to today's Great Lakes State. "Coming to the Lakes," which discusses the migration of people to West Michigan over the last 10,000 years, includes a life-size mastodon, Great Lakes schooner, and more.

Muskegon Heritage Museum

561 W. Western Ave., Muskegon, MI 49440 (43.232947, -86.256666)
(231) 722-1363, www.muskegonheritage.org
Hours: Mid-May to mid-Oct: Thu-Sat 11am-4pm. Also by appointment. *Admission:* Adults $4, Students $2, Children (0-4) free. Group rates available. *Site Info:* Street or city lot parking. Wheelchair accessible. Group and special tours by appointment.

Exhibits at the Muskegon Heritage Museum focus on companies that made Muskegon an industrial capital, as well as the various types of industries: logging, foundries, and manufacturing. Highlights include a working Corliss Valve Steam Engine from the 1890s, an operating Brunswick bowling alley and automatic pinsetter, historic homes exhibit, and a walking tour brochure.

The Scolnik House of the Depression Era

504 W. Clay Ave., Muskegon, MI 49440 (43.232744, -86.255499)
(231) 722-0278, info@lakeshoremuseum.org,
www.lakeshoremuseum.org
Hours: May-Oct: Wed-Sun 12-4pm. Special holiday tours are offered between Thanksgiving and New Year's Day. *Admission:*

Free. *Site Info:* Free street parking. Not wheelchair accessible. Self-guided.

The Scolnik House of the Depression Era was built in the late 1880s in classic Queen Anne-inspired Folk Victorian style. Today, the home features period furnishings, appliances, flooring, and wallpaper, and tells the story of common families living during the Great Depression. A fictional Polish Catholic family owns the two-story home and shares it with a young fictional Polish Jewish family that lives on the second floor.

USS *LST 393* Veterans Museum

506 Mart St., Muskegon, MI 49440 (43.234600, -86.258908)
(231) 730-1477, 82airbn@comcast.net; info@lst393.com,
www.lst393.org
Hours: May-Oct 1: Daily 10am-5pm. *Admission:* Adults $6, Students $4. *Site Info:* Free parking. Partially wheelchair accessible; main deck only. Tour guide available.

The USS *LST 393* is one of only two Landing Ship, Tanks remaining from the 1,051 built during WWII. The ship earned three battle stars during World War II in the invasions of Sicily and Normandy. *LST 393* was then outfitted and painted in camouflage scheme for the intended invasion of Japan. Today, the ship houses the USS *LST 393* Veterans Museum, which honors those who served in America's armed forces and educates the public about their legacy.

USS *Silversides* Submarine Museum

1346 Bluff St., Muskegon, MI 49441 (43.229711, -86.332347)
(231) 755-1230, dherzhaft@silversidesmuseum.org,
www.silversidesmuseum.org
Hours: Jun-Aug: Daily 10am-5:30pm; Sep-May: Sun-Thu 10am-4pm, Fri-Sat 10am-5:30pm. *Admission:* Adults $15, Seniors (62+) $12.50, Children (5-18) $10.50. WWII Veterans, Active Duty, and Children (0-4) free. *Site Info:* Free on-site parking. Wheelchair accessible. Self-guided.

The USS *Silversides* Submarine Museum honors the men and women of the military, preserves military history, and provides experiences that educate the public about military history and technology. The museum includes a wide range of exhibits and displays focusing on the USS *Silversides*, World War II, the Pearl Harbor attack, submarines, the Cold War, marine technology, and Great Lakes shipping. Guests can also opt to tour the actual USS *Silversides* as well as the Coast Guard Cutter *McLane*, a rare Prohibition-era vessel that served from 1927 until 1968.

MUSKEGON HEIGHTS

James Jackson Museum of African American History

7 E. Center St., Muskegon Heights, MI 49444 (43.201781, -86.244169)

(231) 739-9500, Ja2Jck@aol.com, www.facebook.com/Dr.JamesJacksonMuseumofAfricanAmericanHistory

Hours: Mon-Sat 3-5:30pm. *Admission:* Free. *Site Info:* Street parking.

The James Jackson Museum of African American History educates the public about African-American history through exhibits, DVDs, films, literature, etc.

PENTWATER

Pentwater Historical Society Museum

327 S. Hancock St., Pentwater, MI 49449 (43.778695, -86.432988)

c.bigelow@yahoo.com, www.pentwaterhistoricalsociety.org

Hours: Jun-Sep: Mon, Thu, and Sat 2-5pm. *Admission:* Donations accepted. *Site Info:* Street parking or village parking lot. Wheelchair accessible. Self-guided.

The Pentwater Historical Society Museum is located behind and below the Pentwater Village/Township building. The society plans to open its new museum location in the First Baptist Church in the summer of 2014. The society also offers a walking tour that takes visitors to seven different historical interpretive panels throughout the village. Maps are available at the museum and chamber office.

PORTAGE

Air Zoo

6151 Portage Road, Portage, MI 49002 (42.227467, -85.557481)

(269) 382-6555, airzoo@airzoo.org, www.airzoo.org

Hours: Mon-Sat 9am-5pm, Sun 12-5pm. Closed Thanksgiving, Christmas Eve, and Christmas Day. *Admission:* $10. Children (0-4) free. Individual ride tickets are $2 each. *Site Info:* Free on-site parking. Wheelchair accessible. Docents available.

The Air Zoo preserves the legacy of flight for present and future generations. There are more than 80 aircraft on site, where exhibits honor women in aviation and space, commemorate the Guadalcanal campaign during WWII, and celebrate the discoveries of innovators such as Galileo. Guests can also participate in numerous simulations, including a balloon ride, 4-D theater, and 3-D trip to the International Space Station.

*Information may not be current.

ROCKFORD

Algoma Township Historical Society
10531 Algoma Ave., Rockford, MI 49341 (43.156294, -85.6113774)
(616) 866-1583, planning@algomatwp.org, www.algomatwp.org
Hours: Mon-Fri 8:30am-4:30pm. *Admission:* Free. *Site Info:* Free on-site parking. Wheelchair accessible. Self-guided.

The Algoma Township Historical Society maintains rotating history displays in the Algoma Township Hall building.

Oakfield Pioneer Heritage Museum
11009 Podunk Road NE, Rockford, MI 49341 (43.161659, -85.3627985)
(616) 874-6271, jagager@aol.com,
www.commoncorners.com/kent/kent_oakfield_ophs.htm
Hours: Jun-Sep: 2nd and 4th Sat 2-4pm. *Admission:* Donations accepted. *Site Info:* Free on-site parking. Partially wheelchair accessible; main floor only. Tour guide available.

Managed by the Oakfield Pioneer Heritage Society, the Oakfield Pioneer Heritage Museum is located in a former meeting hall of the Ancient Order of Gleaners. Built in 1901, the building now features displays relating to the community's history, including commercial, agricultural, and residential ways of life.

Rockford Area Historical Museum
105 S. Monroe, Rockford, MI 49341 (43.120050, -85.561362)
(616) 866-2235, rockfordmuseum@gmail.com,
www.rockfordmuseum.org
Hours: See website. *Admission:* Free. *Site Info:* Free on-site parking. Wheelchair accessible. Tour guide available. Call ahead to schedule a group tour.

The Rockford Area Historical Museum recently moved into its new home: a former district courthouse adjacent to Rockford City Hall. New exhibits focus on the development of the Rockford area as a logging community and its evolution into a dynamic small city. Other exhibits tell the story of Rockford's business community, schools, connection to America's military history, agriculture, and the nearby townships that comprise the Rockford area.

SAUGATUCK

The Pumphouse Museum
735 Park St., Saugatuck, MI 49453 (42.660635, -86.207147)
(269) 857-5751, fnschmidt@wmol.com, www.sdhistoricalsociety.org

Hours: Memorial Day-Aug: Daily 12-4pm; Sep-Oct: Sat-Sun.
Admission: Donations accepted. *Site Info:* Free on-site parking.

Originally built in 1904 as the city of Saugatuck's first water pumping station, the Pumphouse Museum features changing exhibits that cover everything from shipwrecks and dancing to artists and gangsters. An interactive computer terminal offers topical programs that look at the history of the area's hotels, past residents, and boat building.

SCHOOLCRAFT

Underground Railroad House

613 E. Cass St., Schoolcraft, MI 49087 (42.116127, -85.629694)
(269) 679-4304, schoolcrafthistorical@hotmail.com
Hours: By appointment. *Admission:* $5. *Site Info:* Free on-site parking. Partially wheelchair accessible; first floor only. Tour guide available by appointment.

Schoolcraft's first physician, Dr. Nathan Thomas, reportedly opened his home to more than 1,000 fugitive slaves as they passed through southern Michigan via the Underground Railroad. Operated by the Schoolcraft Historical Society, the Underground Railroad House stands as a tribute to the courage of those who sought to escape slavery and of those who gave aid.

SOUTH HAVEN

Hartman School

355 Hubbard St., South Haven, MI 49090 (42.4018128, -86.2666473)
(269) 637-6424, info@historyofsouthhaven.org,
www.historyofsouthhaven.org
Hours: Memorial Day to Oct: Tue-Wed 9am-4pm, Sun 2-4pm.
Admission: Free. *Site Info:* Free street parking. Wheelchair accessible. Tour guide available on Sundays (Memorial Day through Sep).

The Historical Association of South Haven maintains exhibits and archives in the Hartman School building.

Liberty Hyde Bailey Museum

903 Bailey Ave., South Haven, MI 49090 (42.391020, -86.263822)
(269) 637-3251, lhbm@south-haven.com,
www.libertyhydebailey.org
Hours: May-Sep: Thu-Sun 9am-4pm; Oct-Apr: By appointment.
Admission: Main exhibit is free. Special exhibit is $5 for general public, $3 for seniors/children. *Site Info:* Nearby parking available

for a fee; use hospital parking lot. Partially wheelchair accessible. Tour guide available; groups should call in advance.

The Liberty Hyde Bailey Museum educates people about America's Father of Modern Horticulture through the preservation of his birth site and the promotion of his vision linking horticulture and the environment to everyday life. Constructed in 1857 by Liberty Hyde Bailey Sr., the museum is located in one of the oldest standing homes in South Haven. The main house exhibit takes visitors through Bailey's life story, following his plan of "Learning, Labor, and Leisure."

Michigan Flywheelers Museum

06285 68th St., South Haven, MI 49090 (42.395348, -86.207134)
(269) 639-2010, michiganflywheelers@yahoo.com,
www.michiganflywheelers.org
Hours: Memorial Day to Labor Day: Wed, Sat-Sun 10am-3pm.
Admission: Donations accepted. Admission charged during special events. *Site Info:* Free on-site parking. Wheelchair accessible. Tour guide available.

The Michigan Flywheelers Museum is dedicated to the preservation and education of American farming history and its equipment. Located on 80 acres, the museum offers visitors a look at the lives of the area's early rural settlers. Guests can visit Old Towne, which is filled with businesses and trades that would have been found in the 1920s. Some of the displays include the Old Tyme Jail, Peaceful Knoll Church, and Abbert & Sons Farm Machinery Repair.

Michigan Maritime Museum

260 Dyckman Ave., South Haven, MI 49090 (42.406695, -86.274390)
(269) 637-8078, info@michiganmaritimemuseum.org,
www.michiganmaritimemuseum.org
Hours: See website or call for hours. *Admission:* Adults $6, Seniors $5, Youth $4.50. *Site Info:* Free on-site parking. Partially wheelchair accessible. Self-guided.

The Michigan Maritime Museum preserves and interprets the rich heritage of the Great Lakes, while enhancing the South Haven Maritime District. The museum includes five separate buildings that feature permanent and changing exhibits on Michigan maritime history, a center for the teaching of boat building and related maritime skills, and a regionally renowned research library.

SPARTA

Meyers Schoolhouse Museum

160 E. Division, Sparta, MI 49345 (43.1606364, -85.7061222)

(616) 606-0765, history@spartahistory.org, www.spartahistory.org
Hours: By appointment. *Admission:* Free. *Site Info:* Free on-site parking. Tour guide available.

The Meyers Schoolhouse Museum shows what life was like for students who attended one-room schoolhouses. The museum contains the history of other schools as well as the students who attended Sparta's schools.

ST. JOSEPH

Heritage Museum & Cultural Center
601 Main St., St. Joseph, MI 49085 (42.106252, -86.482407)
*(269) 983-1191, charseneau@theheritagemcc.org,
www.theheritagemcc.org*
Hours: Tue-Sat 10am-4pm. *Admission:* Adults $5, Youth (6-17) $1, Children (0-5) free. *Site Info:* Free on-site parking. Wheelchair accessible. Self-guided.

The Heritage Museum and Cultural Center promotes historical preservation, education, and research that relates to Benton Harbor, St. Joseph, and the surrounding region.

STURGIS

Sturgis Historical Society
200 W. Main St., Sturgis, MI 49091 (41.804696, -85.420278)
(269) 659-2512
Hours: Mon-Fri 8:30am-4:40pm. *Admission:* Donations accepted.
Site Info: Public parking. Not wheelchair accessible.

Built in 1867, the Sturgis Train Depot is now home to the Sturgis Historical Society and Chamber of Commerce.
Information may not be current.

VANDALIA

Bonine House
18970 M-60, Vandalia, MI 49095 (41.919043, -85.933014)
(269) 445-7358, info@urscc.org, www.urscc.org
Hours: Apr-Nov: See website for hours. *Admission:* Donations accepted. *Site Info:* Free on-site parking. Not wheelchair accessible. Tour guide available; donations accepted. Reserve a private group tour by contacting *info@urscc.org*.

Built in 1845 by Quaker abolitionist James E. Bonine, the Bonine House was a classic Greek Revival farmhouse that was remodeled in the Second Empire style after the Civil War. The carriage house across the street sheltered Freedom Seekers on their journey to

Canada, making James and his wife, Sarah, stationmasters on the Underground Railroad. Visit *www.urscc.org* to download a driving tour of Underground Railroad sites throughout Cass County.

VICKSBURG

Vicksburg Historic Village Park

300 N. Richardson St., Vicksburg, MI 49097 (42.122903, -85.530061)
(269) 649-1733, vixmus1@yahoo.com, www.vicksburghistory.org
Hours: May-Dec: Sat 10am-3pm. *Admission:* Free. *Site Info:* Free on-site parking. Partially wheelchair accessible. Tour guide available by appointment; call (269) 649-1733.

The Vicksburg Historic Village Park includes seven buildings: a farm house, barn, school, print shop, town hall, depot, and village garage. Artifacts on display include ice harvest equipment, rolling stock (a caboose, freight, and tank cars), newspapers, photographs, and a Ford Model A.

WHITE CLOUD

Newaygo County Museum and Heritage Center

1099 Wilcox St., White Cloud, MI 49349 (43.419364, -85.799274)
(231) 652-2892, newaygocohistory@yahoo.com, www.ncshg.org
Hours: May-Oct 31: Fri-Sun 12-4pm. *Admission:* Free. *Site Info:* Free street parking. Wheelchair accessible. Tour guide available.

The Newaygo County Museum and Heritage Center features artifacts pertaining to logging, the fur trade, and other activities typical of life in Newaygo County. The museum also features a chronological timeline of Newaygo County's development.

WHITE PIGEON

U.S. Land Office Museum

113 W. Chicago Road, White Pigeon, MI 49099 (41.798315, -85.644017)
(269) 483-7122, mstarmann@yahoo.com,
www.hstarmann.wix.com/sjchs
Hours: By appointment. *Admission:* Donations accepted. *Site Info:* Free street and on-site parking.

Built in 1830, the White Pigeon U.S. Land Office was the third land office in Michigan and, from 1831 to 1834, sold more than 250,000 acres for $1.25 an acre. It is listed in both the State Register of Historic Sites and National Register of Historic Places. The land office houses most of the St. Joseph County Historical Society's collection, which includes 150-year-old primitive tools, toys, instruments, Native American artifacts, and war items.

Wahbememe Memorial Park
Corner of U.S. 12 and U.S. 131,White Pigeon, MI 49099 (41.797103, -85.662503)
(269) 483-7122, mstarmann@yahoo.com,
www.hstarmann.wix.com/sjchs
Hours: Dusk to dawn. *Admission:* Free. *Site Info:* Free on-site parking. Wheelchair accessible. Self-guided.

The mound grave of Potawatomi Chief Wahbememe (White Pigeon), a signer of the 1795 Treaty of Greenville, is listed in the State Register of Historic Sites and National Register of Historic Places. According to legend, Wahbememe ran from Detroit to White Pigeon (nearly 150 miles) after he heard of a plot to attack the settlement. As he did not stop for food or rest, he collapsed from exhaustion and died after warning the village of the possible attack. In 1909, the Alba Columba Club, a White Pigeon women's group, placed the a large stone boulder monument at the site.

WHITEHALL

White River Lighthouse Station
6199 Murray Road, Whitehall, MI 49461 (43.374640, -86.424411)
(231) 845-7417, splkadirector@gmail.com, www.splka.org
Hours: Daily 10am-5pm. *Site Info:* Michigan Recreation Passport is required for entry. Not wheelchair accessible. Self-guided.

Built in 1875, the White River Lighthouse Station was decommissioned in 1960 and opened as a museum in 1970. For a donation of $4/adult and $2/child, visitors can explore the three-room museum and climb the tower.

ZEELAND

New Groningen Schoolhouse
10537 Paw Paw Drive, Zeeland, MI 49464 (42.808110, -86.041124)
(616) 772-4079, info@zeelandmuseum.org, www.zeelandhistory.org
Hours: By appointment. *Site Info:* Wheelchair accessible.

The New Groningen Schoolhouse, built in 1881, is a two-room schoolhouse, complete with desks, maps, school books, and more.

Zeeland Historical Society
37 E. Main Street, Zeeland, MI 49464 (42.812603, -86.0175579)
(616) 772-4079, info@zeelandmuseum.org, www.zeelandhistory.org
Hours: Mar-Oct: Thu 10am-5pm; Year-round: Sat 10am-2pm.
Admission: Free. *Site Info:* Partially wheelchair accessible; film

shown for patrons who cannot travel to second floor. Free parking. Group tours available by appointment; $1/person.

The Zeeland Historical Museum is located in a house and store formerly owned by Dirk Dekker. Restored to its original 1876 style, the building features numerous local history displays as well as a local history resource room. Exhibits cover Dutch immigration, the first Zeeland Bank, farming, and the interurban.

CENTRAL

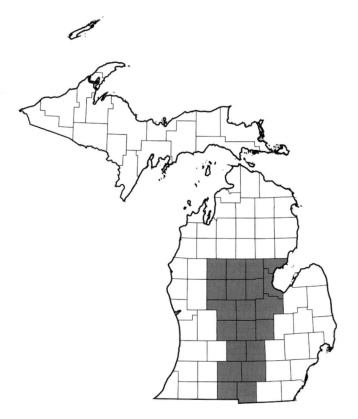

ALBION

Gardner House Museum
509 S. Superior St., Albion, MI 49224 (42.241594, -84.752566)
(517) 629-5100, info@albionhistoricalsociety.org,
www.albionhistoricalsociety.org
Hours: May-Sep: Sat-Sun 2-4pm. Also by appointment. *Admission:*
Donations accepted. *Site Info:* Free street parking. Partially
wheelchair accessible; first floor only. Tour guide available.

Built by local hardware merchant Augustus P. Gardner in 1875, the
Gardner House Museum features period furniture and several
displays relating to Albion's history. A World War II exhibit
showcases uniforms, flags, and 400 photos of Albion residents who
served in the war. Other exhibits include a neighborhood grocery
store, a 19th-century kitchen, and a display featuring school and
church photos from the 1920s.

BATTLE CREEK

Historic Adventist Village

411 Champion St., Battle Creek, MI 49037 (42.327799, -85.197161)
(269) 965-3000, bscherencel@adventistheritage.org,
www.adventistheritage.org
Hours: Sun-Fri 10am-4pm, Sat 2-4pm. *Admission:* Donations
accepted. *Site Info:* Parking lot at corner of West Van Buren and
Wood. Partially wheelchair accessible. Tour guide available;
donations accepted.

Dating back to 1863, the Historic Adventist Village aims to teach
visitors about the history of Battle Creek and the people who once
lived there. The site includes a home that belonged to Harriet
Henderson Tucker (a former slave who escaped through the
Underground Railroad), a log cabin, a one-room schoolhouse, a
1863 church, and more. Also on site is the Dr. John Harvey Kellogg
Discovery Center, which features several of his inventions.

BAY CITY

Historical Museum of Bay County

321 Washington Ave., Bay City, MI 48708 (43.593842, -83.888742)
(989) 893-5733, info@bchsmuseum.org, www.bchsmuseum.org
Hours: Mon-Fri 10am-5pm, Sat 12-4pm. *Admission:* Donations
accepted. *Site Info:* Free parking. Wheelchair accessible. Tour guide
available by appointment.

Active since 1919, the Historical Museum of Bay County is located
in the former National Guard Armory, which was constructed in
1910. The exhibit "Bay County...Trails Through Time" details the
distinctive heritage of Bay County from pre-contact days to the
present. This includes major sections on Native Americans and the
fur trade, lumbering, military history, and local business and
industry. The Kantzler Maritime Gallery details the story of Bay
City's rich maritime history, and the Robert and Ann Hachtel
Theatre features several feature-length documentaries of local and
regional interest.

Trombley-Centre House

901 John F. Kennedy Drive, Bay City, MI 48706 (43.594514,
-83.900114)
(989) 893-5733, info@bchsmuseum.org, www.bchsmuseum.org
Hours: During special events. Also by appointment.

The Trombley/Centre House is the oldest frame house still standing
in Bay County (c. 1840). Today, it includes an heirloom vegetable
garden that features plant varieties from the 1800s and a historic
herb garden. Interpretive signs and a virtual tour are coming soon.

BELDING

Belding Museum at the Historic Belrockton;
Belding Exploration Lab Children's Museum (BEL)
108 Hanover St., Belding, MI 48809 (43.097532, -85.225914)
(616) 794-1900 ex.425,
www.ci.belding.mi.us/pages/community/museum.html
Hours: See website. *Admission:* Free. *Site Info:* Free on-site
parking. Wheelchair accessible. Tour guide available.

Maintained by the Belding Museum Board, Belding Museum at the
Historic Belrockton is located in the 1906 Belrockton Dormitory,
which was once used by single women working at Belding Brothers
& Co. Silk Mill. Themed rooms showcase the old downtown and
include a general store, millinery shop, original "silk girl" bedroom,
and more. Also on site is the Belding Exploration Lab Children's
Museum (BEL), which offers children the opportunity to learn
through creative play and interaction with others. Exhibits include
"Adventure on the Flat," where children can sit in a rowboat that
was manufactured in Belding and "fish" for species native to
Michigan.

Grattan Township Historical Society
12040 Old Belding Road, Belding, MI 48809 (43.084189,
-85.370963)
(616) 826-1872, forcecricket@gmail.com,
www.grattantownship.org/historicalsociety.html
Hours: May-Oct: Sun 2-4pm.

The Grattan Township Historical Society maintains a museum in the
1853 Methodist Episcopal Church, which was used as Grattan
Township Hall until 1971.
*Information may not be current.

BELLEVUE

Bellevue Area Historical Museum
212 N. Main St., Bellevue, MI 49021 (42.445339, -85.018103)
(616) 763-9136, gaddngranny@yahoo.com,
www.rootsweb.com/~mibhs/
Hours: Wed 2-4pm. Also by appointment. *Admission:* Donations
accepted. *Site Info:* Free street parking. Wheelchair accessible. Self-
guided.

Located in Michigan's oldest township library, the Bellevue Area
Historical Museum houses local history and artifacts.

BIG RAPIDS

Jim Crow Museum of Racist Memorabilia
1010 Campus Drive, Big Rapids, MI 49307 (43.687690, -85.482051)
(231) 591-5873, jimcrowmuseum@ferris.edu, www.ferris.edu/jimcrow
Hours: Mon-Fri 8am-5pm. *Admission:* Free. *Site Info:* Wheelchair accessible. Tour guide available; tours for 10 people or more available by appointment. Group tours with children younger than 12 will not be scheduled.

Located in the lower level of Ferris State University's FLITE Library, the Jim Crow Museum of Racist Memorabilia uses objects of intolerance to teach tolerance and promote social justice. It collects, exhibits, and preserves objects and collections related to racial segregation, anti-black caricatures, civil rights, and African American achievement. The museum also offers a comprehensive timeline of the African American experience in the United States.

NOTE: Many of the artifacts and media pieces within the Jim Crow Museum contain explicit images of violence, nudity, offensive language, and other mature themes. Because of this, the museum encourages that all school-age children be accompanied by a guardian or adult. Children younger than 12 must be accompanied by a guardian or adult.

Mecosta County Historical Museum
129 S. Stewart Ave., Big Rapids, MI 49307 (43.697957, -85.478922)
(231) 592-5091, verona705@chartermi.net
Hours: Sat 2-4pm. Also by appointment; call (231) 796-8993. *Admission:* Free. *Site Info:* Street parking. Not wheelchair accessible. Tour guide available by appointment.

Located in the former home of lumberman Fitch Phelps, the Mecosta County Historical Museum showcases historical displays about Mecosta County and the lumber industry.
Information may not be current.

BRECKENRIDGE

Drake House Memorial Museum
328 E. Saginaw St., Breckenridge, MI 48615 (43.407947, -84.475024)
(989) 842-1241, bwahs@yahoo.com, Find on Facebook
Hours: Mon 9am-12pm. *Admission:* Donations accepted. *Site Info:* Free on-site and street parking. Wheelchair accessible. Tour guide available.

Operated by the Breckenridge Wheeler Area Historical Society, the Drake House Memorial Museum is set in the 1920s era. It includes a doctor's office featuring medical instruments that were used from 1920 to 1950. There is also a carriage house on site.

Plank Road Museum
404 E. Saginaw St., Breckenridge, MI 48615 (43.4079571, -84.4747135)
(989) 842-1241, bwahs@yahoo.com, Find on Facebook
Hours: Mon 9am-12pm. *Admission:* Donations accepted. *Site Info:* Free on-site and street parking. Wheelchair accessible. Tour guide available.

Operated by the Breckenridge-Wheeler Area Historical Society, the Plank Road Museum is located in a Baptist church that was built in 1890. Exhibits change on an annual basis.

BROOKLYN

Walker Tavern Historic Complex
13220 M-50, Brooklyn, MI 49230 (42.063711, -84.223656)
(517) 241-0731, museuminfo@michigan.gov,
www.michigan.gov/walkertavern
Hours: See website. *Admission:* Free. *Site Info:* Free on-site parking. Partially wheelchair accessible. Self-guided.

In the mid-19th century, a stagecoach ride from Detroit to Chicago was a long and arduous five-day trip. Discover Michigan's agricultural and travel heritage through Sylvester Walker's stagecoach stop at a historic crossroads.

CHARLOTTE

1845 Eaton County Courthouse
1305 S. Cochran Ave., Charlotte, MI 48813 (42.546516, -84.834280)
(517) 543-6999, csamuseum@yahoo.com,
www.csamuseum.weebly.com/index.html
Hours: By appointment. *Admission:* Varies. *Site Info:* Free on-site parking. Wheelchair accessible. Self-guided.

Located in Bennett Park, this former Eaton County Courthouse is restored to the 1845 time period.

Eaton County's Museum at Courthouse Square
100 W. Lawrence Ave., Charlotte, MI 48813 (42.563977, -84.835951)
(517) 543-6999, csamuseum@yahoo.com,
www.csamuseum.weebly.com/index.html

Hours: Tue-Thu 9am-4pm. *Admission:* $1. *Site Info:* Free on-site parking. Partially wheelchair accessible; second and third floors require assistance. Tour guide available; call ahead for large groups.

Built from 1882 to 1885, the Eaton County Courthouse was used until 1976. Today, it is home to Eaton County's Museum at Courthouse Square, which features 10 exhibit rooms covering the history of Eaton County, the military, and more.

CHESANING

Chesaning Historical Museum
602 W. Broad St., Chesaning, MI 48047 (43.186314, -84.120706)
(989) 845-3155, cahs@centurytel.net, www.cahs.chesaning.com
Hours: Temporarily closed; expected reopening in May 2014. Call for details. *Admission:* Free. *Site Info:* Street parking. Wheelchair accessible. Tour guide available.

Displays and permanent exhibits at the Chesaning Historical Museum focus on the area's history from Native American habitations to present-day local businesses, industries, schools, etc.

CLARE

Clare County Museum Complex
7050 S. Eberhart Ave., Clare, MI 48617 (43.886882, -84.747773)
(734) 755-2638, museum@clarecountyhistory.org,
www.clarecountyhistory.org
Hours: May to mid-Oct: Sat 1-4pm. Also by appointment.
Admission: Donations accepted. *Site Info:* Free on-site and street parking. Wheelchair accessible. Tour guide available during open hours and by appointment.

The Clare County Museum Complex includes three buildings. The Clare County Museum has history exhibits about Native Americans, the military, loggers and logging railroads, ghost towns, and Spikehorn Meyer (a county showman and animal handler). The one-room Dover Schoolhouse has displays relating to one-room schools at the early 20th century and artifacts relating to Clare County schools.

COLDWATER

Quincy One-room School House
262 S. Sprague St., Coldwater, MI 49036 (41.931721, -84.990651)
(517) 278-2871, bchistorybook@aol.com,
www.branchcountyhistoricalsociety.org
Hours: Open during Branch County Fair Week. Also by appointment. *Admission:* Donations accepted. *Site Info:* Free street

parking. Not wheelchair accessible. Tour guide available.

Originally located in Quincy, the 1846 One-room School House was moved to the Branch County Fairgrounds and restored to represent the classroom accommodations that children experienced in the mid-1800s. In 2012, the Branch County Historical Society received an award from the Michigan One-room Schoolhouse Association for the most improved restoration of such a structure.

Wing House Museum
27 S. Jefferson St., Coldwater, MI 49036 (41.939395, -84.997614)
(517) 278-2871, bchistorybook@aol.com,
www.branchcountyhistoricalsociety.org
Hours: 3rd Sat monthly 12-4pm. Also by appointment. *Admission:* Minimum donation of $3/person. *Site Info:* Free street parking. Not wheelchair accessible. Tour guide available.

Constructed in 1875 for newlyweds Jay and Frances Chandler, the Wing House Museum is an example of Second Empire architecture with a convex mansard roof. In 1882, the house was purchased by the Wing family, who owned it until 1974. Since then, the house has been restored to reflect the presence of both the Chandler and Wing families. Most of the furnishings on display in the museum belonged to the two families, some dating back to the mid-1800s.

CONCORD

Mann House
205 Hanover St., Concord, MI 49237 (42.177479, -84.643312)
(517) 373-3559, museuminfo@michigan.gov,
www.michigan.gov/mannhouse
Hours: May 27-Sep 2: Thu-Sun 10am-4pm. Call or check website to confirm. *Admission:* Free. *Site Info:* Free street parking. Not wheelchair accessible. Self-guided.

In 1883, Daniel and Ellen Mann built a two-story house in the small, picturesque farming community of Concord. Today, the Mann house features eight rooms of period furniture, including pieces from the 1840s to the early 20th century. The site is also home to restored flower and herb gardens, a carriage house with carriages and sleighs, and exhibits that illustrate the way Michiganians worked and played in the 19th and 20th centuries.

DURAND

Michigan Railroad History Museum
200 Railroad St., Durand, MI 48429 (42.909385, -83.982313)
(989) 288-3561, dusi@durandstation.org, www.durandstation.org
Hours: Tue-Thu 1-5pm, Fri-Sat 10am- 5pm, Sun 1-5pm. *Admission:*

Free. *Site Info:* On-site parking. Wheelchair accessible. Tour guide available; group tours by appointment.

Located in the Durand Union Station, the Michigan Railroad History Museum collects, preserves, and interprets artifacts, records, and documents related to the history of railroads and railroading in Michigan. It engages in activities that encourage interest in the railroad industry and is a source of information on railroad groups and structures throughout Michigan.
Information may not be current.

EAST LANSING

Michigan State University Museum
409 W. Circle Drive, East Lansing, MI 48824 (42.731545, -84.481699)
(517) 355-2370, pr@museum.msu.edu, www.museum.msu.edu
Hours: Mon-Fri 9am-5pm, Sat 10am-5pm, Sun 1-5pm. Closed university holidays. *Admission:* $5 suggested donation. *Site Info:* Parking in front of building; $1 for two-hour permit. Wheelchair accessible.

Organized in 1857, the Michigan State University Museum is a resource for natural and cultural history, particularly of the Great Lakes region. Exhibits at the museum include a country store, a print shop, and a Michigan fur trade display.

EATON RAPIDS

The Miller Farm
635 State St., Eaton Rapids, MI 48827 (42.509762, -84.643585)
(517) 256-9460, info@eatonrapidshistory.com,
www.eatonrapidshistory.weebly.com
Hours: Wed 10am-5pm. *Admission:* Donations accepted. *Site Info:* Free on-site parking. Partially wheelchair accessible. Tour guide available by appointment.

The Miller Farm is the former home of Miller Dairy, which helped make Eaton Rapids "Ice Cream Capital of the World" for many years. Now listed in the State Register of Historic Sites, the farm includes several historic buildings and one of Michigan's largest barns, which showcases a full hay loft and historical displays. The former Miller Dairy Ice Cream factory includes an eclectic museum and a 1950s-era ice cream parlor that is open every weekend to the public.

ESSEXVILLE

Heritage House Farm Museum
305 Pine St., Essexville, MI 48732 (43.606209, -83.837171)
(989) 686-7025, lenglehardt7025@charter.net,
pranspaugh@yahoo.com, www.theheritagemcc.org
Hours: Summer: Sun 2-4pm. Also by appointment. *Admission:*
Donations accepted. *Site Info:* Not wheelchair accessible. Nearby
parking available. Tours by appointment only.

The Heritage House Farm Museum is a fully furnished nine-room
home from the early 1890s. The home was built by John Garber,
whose family members were the building's only residents. Today,
the home features furniture that belonged to both the Garber family
and the community. Also on site are a German-style shed, corn crib,
and herb garden.

EVART

Evart Public Library Museum
105 N. Main St., Evart, MI 49631 (43.900876, -85.259410)
(231) 734-5542
Hours: Mon 9am-6pm, Tue-Fri 9am-4pm. *Admission:* Free. *Site
Info:* Street and lot parking. Wheelchair accessible. Call ahead for
tour guide availability.

The Evart Public Library Museum collects artifacts, records, and
archival materials that document and/or illustrate local history.
Rotating exhibits and freestanding items relate to the history of the
Evart area and the interests of its citizens.

FARWELL

Farwell Area Historical Museum
221 W. Main St., Farwell, MI 48430 (43.835180, -84.868681)
(989) 588-0580, trishtom68@yahoo.com, www.farwellmuseum.com
Hours: Year-round: Thu-Fri 12-4pm; Summer: Sat 12-4pm.
Admission: Free. *Site Info:* Free on-site and street parking.
Wheelchair accessible. Free tour guide available.

The Farwell Area Historical Society maintains a museum in the
1882 Ladies Library Association building. Exhibits highlight local
history and include school, mill, post office, and local figures.

FOWLERVILLE

Livingston Centre Historical Village
8800 W. Grand River Ave., Fowlerville, MI 48836 (42.661082,

-84.089229)
(517) 223-8186, jrhodes@fowlervillefamilyfair.com,
www.fowlervillefamilyfair.com
Hours: By appointment or during fairground events. *Admission:*
Donations accepted. *Site Info:* Free on-site parking. Partially
wheelchair accessible. Tour guide available by appointment.

The Livingston Centre Historical Village is home to eight buildings,
including the 1910 Hartland Barber Shop, the 1906 Iosco Methodist
Episcopal Church, and the 1870 Clinton Shoe Repair & Harness
Shop. The Pere Marquette Depot, built in 1872, is home to several
model train displays.

FRANKENMUTH

Frankenmuth Historical Association Museum
613 S. Main St., Frankenmuth, MI 48734 (43.328206, -83.739420)
(989) 652-9701, fhaoffice@airadv.net,
www.frankenmuthmuseum.org
Hours: Mon-Thu 10am-5pm, Fri-Sat 10am-7pm, Sun 12-6pm.
Admission: Adults $2, Students $1, Family $5. Price includes
admission to Lager Mill Museum. *Site Info:* Free public parking.
Wheelchair accessible. Self-guided.

Built in 1905, the former Kern Commercial House Hotel now serves
as the Frankenmith Historical Association Museum, which focuses
on the history of Frankenmuth. Exhibits change quarterly.

Lager Mill Brewing Museum
701 Mill St., Frankenmuth, MI (43.325899, -83.741287)
(989) 652-3377, fhaoffice@airadv.net,
www.frankenmuthmuseum.org
Hours: Mon-Thu 11am-7pm, Fri-Sat 10am-9pm, Sun 12-6pm.
Admission: Adults $2, Students $1, Family $5. Price includes
admission to Frankenmuth Historical Association Museum. *Site
Info:* Free on-site parking. Wheelchair accessible. Self-guided.

The Lager Mill Brewing Museum shares Frankenmuth's brewing
heritage and explores the brewing process. The two-story brewing
museum is housed in the historic Nickless-Hubinger Flour Mill
along the Cass River. Displays include antique signs, glasses, and
bottles.

Michigan's Own Military & Space Museum
1250 Weiss St., Frankenmuth, MI 48734 (43.318247, -83.735212)
(989) 652-8005, michown@ejourney.com,
www.michigansmilitarymuseum.com
Hours: Mar-Dec: Sat-Sun 10am-5pm. *Admission:* Adults $5,
Seniors (65+) $4, Students (6-18) $2, Children (0-6) free. *Site Info:*
Parking available. Wheelchair accessible. Tour guide available.

Michigan's Own Military & Space Museum honors Michigan soldiers, sailors, and aviators who fought in our nation's seven foreign wars, from the Spanish-American War through the War on Terror. It also includes exhibits devoted to astronauts who are native to Michigan, the state's former governors, and the world's largest Medal of Honor collection.
Information may not be current.

GLADWIN

Gladwin County Historical Museum
221 W. Cedar Ave., Gladwin, MI 48624 (43.980679, -84.488435)
(989) 426-9277, www.gladwinhistory.org
Hours: Thu-Sat 10am-4pm. *Admission:* Free. *Site Info:* Free on-site parking. Wheelchair accessible; use rear entrance. Tour guide available; donations accepted.

Attractions at the Gladwin County Historical Museum include antiques belonging to the first families, WWI memorabilia, a square grand piano from the 1850s, an antique barbershop, a portable embalming table and tools, and antique hand tools.

Gladwin County Historical Village
515 E. Cedar Ave., Gladwin, MI 48624 (43.980619, -84.481165)
(989) 426-9277, www.gladwinhistory.org
Hours: Memorial Day to Labor Day: Sat 10am-4pm. *Admission:* Free. *Site Info:* Free parking. Wheelchair accessible.

The Gladwin County Historical Village includes a restored Michigan Central Railroad depot and seven other buildings.

GRAND LEDGE

Grand Ledge Area Historical Society Museum
118 W. Lincoln St., Grand Ledge, MI 48837 (42.751964, -84.748702)
(517) 627-5170, marnor1@comcast.net, www.gdledgehistsoc.org
Hours: Tue 10am-12pm, Sun 2-4pm, Festival Days 12-4pm. Also by appointment. *Admission:* Donations accepted. *Site Info:* Street and church parking lot behind building. Wheelchair accessible. Tour guide available; $25 by special arrangement.

Housed in an 1880 Gothic Revival house, the Grand Ledge Area Historical Society Museum changes its themed exhibit each year. It has a large collection of local artifacts relating to the Grand Ledge Chair Company, Grand Ledge Clay products, businesses, farming, artists, and school history.

GRASS LAKE

Dewey School
11501 Territorial Road, Grass Lake, MI 48340 (42.411515, -84.190355)
(517) 596-2254, info@waterloofarmmuseum.org,
www.waterloofarmmuseum.org
Hours: By appointment. *Admission:* Adults $5; memberships available. *Site Info:* Free on-site parking. Not wheelchair accessible. Tour guide available by appointment.

The Dewey School is a 19th-century one-room schoolhouse.

Waterloo Farm Museum
13493 Waterloo Munith Road, Grass Lake, MI 49240 (42.379327, -84.180657)
(517) 596-2254, info@waterloofarmmuseum.org,
www.waterloofarmmuseum.org
Hours: Memorial Day to Labor Day: Weekends. *Admission:* Adults $5. *Site Info:* Free on-site parking. Partially wheelchair accessible. Tour guide available; cost included in admission.

The Waterloo Area Historical Society educates the public about pioneer Michigan farming life and history. The Waterloo Farm Museum includes several buildings, such as the farmhouse, the Really Barn, milk house, log cabin, workshop/forge, ice house, and more. Attractions include a 1850s brick and wood frame farm house, barns, a 1840s log house, and an 1880s one-room school.

Whistlestop Park & Grass Lake Depot
210 E. Michigan, Grass Lake, MI 49240 (42.251565, -84.211781)
(517) 522-4384, jojumac2@yahoo.com, www.grasslakechamber.org
Hours: Tours by appointment. *Admission:* Donations accepted. *Site Info:* Parking on Main Street. Wheelchair accessible.

In 1887, the Michigan Central Railroad replaced its Grass Lake depot with a stone building designed by Detroit architectural firm Spier & Rohns using stone from a quarry at Foster's Station. Today, the depot features artwork and artifacts.

GREENVILLE

Fighting Falcon Military Museum
516 W. Cass St., Greenville, MI 48838 (43.178567, -85.260264)
(616) 225-1940, www.thefightingfalcon.org
Hours: Apr-Nov: Sun 2-4pm. Also by appointment. *Admission:* Donations accepted. *Site Info:* Free on-site and street parking. Wheelchair accessible. Tour guide available during open hours and by appointment.

Located in a restored school building from 1902, the Fighting Falcon Military Museum maintains a collection of military artifacts. Its main exhibit concerns the restoration of the U.S. Army Air Corps CG4A *Fighting Falcon,* which was made locally by the Gibson Refrigerator Company. The primary focus of the museum's exhibits centers on WWII, but artifacts from the Civil War, WWI, Korean War, Vietnam, and modern conflicts are also displayed.

HANOVER

Conklin Reed Organ and History Museum
105 Fairview St., Hanover, MI 49241 (42.102380, -84.547558)
(517) 563-8927, hhahs@frontier.com,
www.conklinreedorganmuseum.org
Hours: May-Oct : Sun 1-5pm. Also by appointment. *Admission:* Donations accepted. *Site Info:* On-site parking. Partially wheelchair accessible. Self-guided. Group tours for 10 or more people available by appointment; cost is $3/person.

Housed in a 1911 Quincy Box style schoolhouse, the Conklin Reed Organ and History Museum displays a collection of more than 100 playable reed (pump) organs, melodeons, and harmoniums. Other attractions include a restored antique fire apparatus, 1950s-era water pump truck, restored classroom, printing press, and Ford Model-T popcorn truck. Listed in the National Register of Historic Places, the museum also offers organ restoration workshops that give hands-on training in reed organ repair and maintenance.

HILLSDALE

Hillsdale County Fairgrounds Museum
115 S. Broad St., Hillsdale 49242 (41.914797, -84.627814)
(517) 547-7784, linc.jomiller@comcast.net,
www.hillsdalehistoricalsociety.org
Admission: Free. *Hours:* Last week of Sep: 10am-8pm. *Site Info:* Free street parking. Wheelchair accessible. Tour guide available.

The Hillsdale County Fairgrounds Museum features a 1920s kitchen, pump organ, and player piano. Exhibits change on an annual basis.

Will Carleton Poorhouse
180 N. Wolcott St., Hillsdale, MI 49242 (41.9227315, -84.6167395)
(517) 547-7784, linc.jomiller@comcast.net,
www.hillsdalehistoricalsociety.org
Hours: By appointment. *Admission:* Free. *Site Info:* Free on-site parking. Partially wheelchair accessible. Tour guide available with advance registration on website; donations accepted.

Built in 1853 by Isaac Vandenbergh, this cobblestone structure was once used as the Hillsdale County Poorhouse from 1854 to 1867 and was the basis for Will Carleton's poem "Over the Hill to the Poor House." Also on site is a partially restored barn, part of which was built in the mid-1800s, containing buggies and a sleigh. There is also a henhouse that has been converted into a general store exhibit.

HOMER

Blair Historical Farm
26445 E. M-60, Homer, MI 49245 (42.155240, -84.780938)
(517) 568-3116, joanne.miller43@gmail.com,
www.homerchamber.org/Homer_Historical_Society.asp
Hours: By appointment. *Admission:* Donations accepted. *Site Info:*
Free on-site parking. Wheelchair accessible. Tour guide available by appointment.

The Homer Historical Society maintains Blair Historical Farm, a pioneer family farm with a barn and outbuildings. Originally owned by Homer's first pioneer doctor, George Blair, the property also features the former Albion town hall and Grover railroad depot—both of which were moved to the farm and renovated for use as display areas.

HUBBARDSTON

Hubbardston Area Historical Society Museum
305 Russell St., Hubbardston, MI 48845 (43.096593, -84.840610)
hubb.northplains@gmail.com, www.hubbardston.org
Hours: Tue-Wed 2-4pm. Also by appointment; call (989) 584-3803.
Admission: Donations accepted. *Site Info:* Free on-site parking.
Wheelchair accessible. Tour guide available.

Located in the local community center (the former public elementary school), the Hubbardston Area Historical Society Museum displays family histories, photographs, township histories, and property and registration records from Ionia, Clinton, Montcalm, and Gratiot counties. Attractions include a Hubbardston Mill tool display, an original Methodist church pump organ, and more.

St. John the Baptist Catholic Church Complex
324 S. Washington St., Hubbardston, MI 48845 (43.091225, -84.845121)
hubb.northplains@gmail.com, www.hubbardston.org
Hours: By appointment; call Joanne Howard at (989) 584-3803.
Admission: Donations accepted. *Site Info:* Free on-site parking.
Wheelchair accessible. Self-guided.

Built in 1868, St. John the Baptist Catholic Church sat 400 people, making it the largest building in Ionia County at the time. It features 17 stained-glass windows, which were installed in 1905 and registered with the Michigan Stained Glass Census in late 1990s. Other buildings on site include the rectory (b.1907) and a former school (b.1919). The cemetery, which was dedicated in 1884, is still in use today.

IONIA

John C. Blanchard House
251 E. Main St., Ionia, MI 48846 (42.983204, -85.057662)
(616) 527-6281, kknoop@charter.net, www.ioniahistory.org
Hours: Jun-Aug and Dec: Sun 1-4pm. Also by appointment.
Admission: $3 suggested donation. *Site Info:* On-site and street parking. Not wheelchair accessible. Tour guide available.

Built in 1881, this fully restored mansion was once home to John C. Blanchard. Today, the building is furnished with rare antiques, and its basement serves as the area's local museum.

ITHACA

Gratiot County Area Historical Museum
129 W. Center St., Ithaca, MI 48847 (43.291482, -84.608979)
(989) 875-6232, carol@gchgs.org, www.gchgs.org
Hours: Tue 12-3 pm. *Admission:* Free. *Site Info:* Free street parking. Wheelchair accessible. Tour guide available.

The Gratiot County Area Historical Museum is located in a red brick Victorian house that was built it 1881 and is listed in the State Register of Historic Sites. It features a collection of furniture reflecting styles of the 19th and 20th centuries. A small, on-site barn features many farm implements and tools, a closed buggy, and an open farm wagon.
Information may not be current.

JACKSON

Ella Sharp Museum of Art & History
3225 Fourth St., Jackson, MI 49203 (42.214907, -84.418108)
(517) 787-2320, judyh@ellasharp.org, www.ellasharp.org
Hours: Tue-Wed 10am-5pm, Thu 10am-7pm, Fri-Sat 10am-5pm.
Admission: Adults $3-$7, Children (5-12) $3-$5, Children (0-4) free. *Site Info:* Free on-site parking. Wheelchair accessible. Tour guide available; farmhouse tours by appointment.

The Ella Sharp Museum of Art & History promotes the understanding and appreciation of art and history through exhibits, interpretation of historical buildings, and educational programs. Ella Sharp Park includes Ella Sharp's 19th-century Hillside Farmhouse, the Dibble One-Room Schoolhouse, Eli Stilson's Log House, and the Merriman-Sharp Tower Barn. Six galleries feature changing exhibits of art and Jackson history.

LANSING

Turner-Dodge House

100 E. North St., Lansing, MI 48906 (42.751631, -84.552530)
(517) 483-4220, DodgeTurner@gmail.com,
http://parks.cityoflansingmi.com/tdodge
Hours: Tue-Fri 10am-5pm. *Admission:* Lansing Residents $3.50, Non-residents $5, Children $2. *Site Info:* Partially wheelchair accessible; first floor only. Offers a complete video-guided tour of the home. Several guided tour packages; call or e-mail for pricing.

James Turner built the Turner-Dodge House in 1858. From 1900 to 1903, his daughter Abby and son-in-law Frank Dodge expanded the home. The expansion included a first-floor kitchen, additional bedrooms to the second floor, and a third-floor ballroom.
*Information may not be current.

Michigan Historical Museum

702 W. Kalamazoo, Lansing, MI 48909 (42.732098, -84.563000)
(517) 373-3559, museuminfo@michigan.gov,
www.michigan.gov/museum
Hours: Mon-Fri 9am-4:30pm, Sat 10am-4pm, Sun 1-5pm.
Admission: Adults $6, Seniors $4, Youth (5-17) $2, Children (0-5) free. *Site Info:* On-site parking; $1/hour on weekdays, free on weekends. Wheelchair accessible. Self-guided.

The Michigan Historical Museum is the flagship of Michigan's state museum system and includes five levels featuring 26 exhibits. The museum surrounds visitors with Michigan history from the time of its earliest people to the late 20th century. Mini-versions of some of the past special exhibits can be accessed on the museum's website.

Michigan Women's Historical Center & Hall of Fame

213 W. Malcolm X St., Lansing, MI 48933 (42.725142, -84.554702)
(517) 484-1880, info@michiganwomen.org,
www.michiganwomenshalloffame.org
Hours: Wed-Sat 12-4pm. Also 1st Sun monthly 2-4pm. Closed holidays. *Admission:* Adults $2.50, Seniors $2, Students $1. *Site Info:* On-site parking. Wheelchair accessible. Tour guide available.

Opened in 1987 by the Michigan Women's Studies Association, the Michigan Women's Historical Center & Hall of Fame was the nation's first state-level facility to focus on women's history. The center offers exhibits that celebrate the achievements and history of Michigan women, including members of the Michigan Women's Hall of Fame. It also contains an art gallery with changing exhibits displaying the work of female artists from Michigan.

R.E. Olds Transportation Museum

240 Museum Drive, Lansing, MI 48933 (42.731533, -84.547891)
(517) 372-0529, director@reoldsmuseum.org,
www.reoldsmuseum.org
Hours: Jan-Dec: Tue-Sat 10am-5pm; April-Oct: Sun 12-5pm.
Admission: Adults $6, Seniors (65+) $4, Students $4, Family (same household) $12. *Site Info:* Free on-site and street parking. Wheelchair accessible. Tour guide available; $3/person.

The R.E. Olds Transportation Museum collects, preserves, studies, and interprets objects that illustrate the part Lansing played in the development of transportation. It places emphasis on the automobile and its effect on Lansing and its people. On display are 50+ cars and trucks, a Curved Dash Olds assembly line display, the first automobile built by R.E. Olds, and an EV1 electric car.

MARSHALL

Capitol Hill School

602 Washington St., Marshall, MI 49068 (42.2648504, -84.9521652)
(269) 781-8544, www.marshallhistoricalsociety.org
Admission: $3. *Site Info:* Free on-site parking. Wheelchair accessible. Tour guide available by appointment; additional costs may apply for groups of fewer than 20 people.

Built in 1860, Capitol Hill School is a two-room schoolhouse that served the city for 101 years. The Gothic Revival building was removed from public service in 1961, but continues to provide a turn-of-the-century classroom experience. The Capitol Hill School is listed in the National Register of Historic Places and the Historical American Building Survey.

G.A.R. Hall

402 E. Michigan Ave., Marshall, MI 49068 (42.271862, -84.954936)
(269) 781-8544, www.marshallhistoricalsociety.org
Hours: May 1-Oct 31: Sat 1-4pm. *Admission:* $3. *Site Info:* Free on-site parking. Wheelchair accessible. Tour guide available; additional costs may apply for tours during off-season hours.

Built in 1902, the G.A.R. Hall currently houses Marshall memorabilia, including items from the Civil War and Spanish-American War as well as police and firefighter artifacts.

Honolulu House Museum

107 N. Kalamazoo Ave., Marshall, MI 49068 (42.272720, -84.964533)
(269) 781-8544, www.marshallhistoricalsociety.org
Hours: May 1-Oct 31: Daily 11am-5pm. Call or see website for off-season hours. *Admission:* $5. *Site Info:* Free on-site parking. Partially wheelchair accessible. Elevator may be inaccessible in 2013 due to renovations; call ahead to check status. Tour guide available; additional costs may apply for tours during off-season hours.

The Honolulu House was built in 1860 by Abner Pratt, then-consul to the Sandwich Islands. The exterior architecture is a blend of Italianate, Gothic, and Polynesian. The interior is restored to the splendor of the 1880s and includes period furnishings and authentic replicas of the carpets. The Honolulu House Museum is listed in the National Register of Historic Places and the Historical American Building Survey.

Walters Gasoline Museum

220 W. Michigan Ave., Marshall, MI 49068 (42.272042, -84.961589)
(269) 789-2562, dwalters@waltersdimmick.com
Hours: May-Oct 1: Sat-Sun 1-4pm. Also by appointment; call (269) 781-4654, ext. 562. *Admission:* Free. *Site Info:* Free on-site parking. Not wheelchair accessible. Tour guide available.

Walter's Gasoline Museum teaches the public about the history of Marshall, Calhoun County, and the state of Michigan. The museum features photos of the Marshall Interurban Railroad that ran through downtown Marshall and a map of the routes once used by the interurban in Michigan. Across the parking lot from the museum is a mural that depicts Marshall's railway station, depot, and first gasoline station.

MASON

Ingham County Courthouse

341 S. Jefferson St., Mason, 48854 (42.579697, -84.442232)
(517) 676-7200, bbennett@ingham.org, http://bc.ingham.org
Hours: By appointment. Closed Wed. *Admission:* Free. *Site Info:* Free parking. Wheelchair accessible. Tour guide available.

Completed in 1904, the current Ingham County Courthouse was put in the National Register of Historic Places in 1971.

Mason Historical Museum

200 E. Oak St., Mason, MI 48854 (42.577902, -84.441063)
(517) 697-9837, www.masonmuseum.com
Hours: Tue, Thu, and Sat 1-3pm. *Admission:* Free. *Site Info:* Street
parking. Wheelchair accessible. Tour guide available during open
hours or by appointment.

The Mason Area Historical Society Museum features exhibits and
artifacts related to the history of Mason.

The Pink School

707 W. Ash, Mason, MI 48854 (42.57837, -84.455143)
(517) 697-9837, www.masonmuseum.com
Hours: By appointment. *Admission:* Free. *Site Info:* Street parking.
Wheelchair accessible. Tours available by appointment.

The one-room Pink School originally opened in 1854. It displays old
school memorabilia, records of teachers, etc.

MIDLAND

Alden B. Dow Home & Studio

315 Post St., Midland, MI 48640 (43.623320, -84.254125)
(866) 315-7678, info@abdow.org, www.abdow.org
Hours: Tours are held Feb-Dec: Mon-Sat 2pm, Fri-Sat 10am.
Admission: Adults $15, Seniors (62+) $12, Students $7. *Site Info:*
Free on-site parking. Not wheelchair accessible.

The Alden B. Dow Home & Studio was the home of Alden B. Dow,
an organic architect. Today, his home and studio is a National
Historic Landmark that is open for tours and educational
programming. It houses original furnishings, a ceramic and glass
collection from the 1930s-1960s, personal and professional libraries,
historic model-scale trains, and mechanical toys.

Chippewa Nature Center

400 S. Badour Road, Midland, MI 48640 (43.600501, -84.293251)
(517) 631-0830, kbagnall@chippewanaturecenter.org,
www.chippewanaturecenter.org
Hours: Mon-Fri 8am-5pm, Sat 9am-5pm, Sun and Holidays 1-4 pm.
Admission: Free. *Site Info:* Free on-site parking. Wheelchair
accessible. Self-guided.

The visitor center at the Chippewa Nature Center provides hands-on
exhibits about the natural and cultural history of the area. On
Sunday afternoons from Memorial Day through Labor Day, visitors
can tour the reconstructed 1870s Homestead Farm and Log

Schoolhouse, and participate in historical chores, games, and activities. In March, visitors can visit the log sugarhouse, watch maple syrup making, and tour the nearby sugarbush.

Midland County Historical Society Heritage Park

3417 W. Main Street, Midland, MI 48640 (43.628857, -84.266078)
(989) 631-5930 x. 1601, info@mcfta.org, www.mcfta.org
Hours: Wed-Sat 11am-4pm. *Admission:* Adults $5, Youth (4-14) $3, Children (0-3) free. *Site Info:* On-site parking. Wheelchair accessible. Guided group tours available by appointment.

The Midland County Historical Society Heritage Park is home to the Herbert D. Doan Midland County History Center, which offers the Midland History Gallery and hands-on interactive exhibits. Also on site is the Herbert H. Dow Historical Museum, which chronicles the life of the Dow Chemical Co. and details the many inventions created in Midland. The 1874 Bradley Home Museum and Carriage House, one of Michigan's only hands-on historic house museums, has Victorian furnishings, fixtures, and costumes.
Information may not be current.

MOUNT PLEASANT

1901 Bohannon Schoolhouse

West Campus Drive and Preston Street, Mount Pleasant, MI 48859 (43.589890, -84.769060)
(989) 774-3829, cmuseum@cmich.edu, www.museum.cmich.edu
Hours: By appointment. *Admission:* Free. *Site Info:* Parking in Lot 22. Wheelchair accessible.

The restored 1901 Bohannon Schoolhouse is open by appointment for tours, which are conducted by Central Michigan University students studying museum studies and/or public history.

Clarke Historical Library

Central Michigan University Library, Park 142, Mount Pleasant, MI 48859 (43.589763, -84.774199)
(989) 774-3352, clarke@cmich.edu, www.clarke.cmich.edu
Hours: Mon-Fri 8am-5pm. *Admission:* Free. *Site Info:* Metered parking. Wheelchair accessible.

Located on the first floor of the Charles V. Park Library, the Clarke Historical Library features two exhibits each year. Past exhibits, which highlight some aspect of the library's collections, have included topics such as the French in Michigan, the Ann Arbor Railroad, Hemingway's Michigan, the state's oil and gas industry, and the history of newspapers in Michigan.

Mount Pleasant Area Historical Society

200 N. Main St., Mount Pleasant, MI 48858 (43.605554, -84.776648)

(989) 854-2509, mtpleasantmiareahistoricalsociety@charter.net, www.mifamilyhistory.org/isabella/MPHistoricalSociety

The Mount Pleasant Area Historical Society maintains rotating exhibits pertaining to Isabella County's history in the lobby of the Isabella County Building.

Museum of Cultural & Natural History

Central Michigan University, 103 Rowe Hall, Mount Pleasant, MI 48859 (43.592972, -84.769665)

(989) 774-3829, cmuseum@cmich.edu, www.museum.cmich.edu
Hours: Mon-Fri 8am-5pm, Sat-Sun 1-5pm. *Admission:* Suggested donation of $1/adult and $0.50/child. *Site Info:* Metered parking or parking passes available. Wheelchair accessible. Tour guides available by appointment; suggested donations vary.

A unit of Central Michigan University, the Museum of Cultural & Natural History features exhibits relating to prehistoric glaciers and mastodons, Native Americans and fur traders, and Civil War soldiers and lumbermen.

Ziibiwing Center of Anishinabe Culture & Lifeways

6650 E. Broadway, Mount Pleasant, MI 48858 (43.602774, -84.713719)

(989) 775-4750, aheard@sagchip.org, www.sagchip.org/ziibiwing
Hours: Mon-Sat 10am-6pm. *Admission:* Adults $6.50, Seniors $3.75, Students $4.50, Youth $3.75, Children (0-4) free. *Site Info:* On-site parking. Wheelchair accessible. Tour guide available.

The Ziibiwing Center of Anishinabe Culture & Lifeways is an American Indian museum that includes the permanent exhibit "Diba Jimooyung" (Telling Our Story), changing exhibit areas, collections storage area, and research center. The exhibits teach visitors about the history, culture, and contemporary society of the Saginaw Chippewa Indian Tribe and other Great Lakes Anishinabek.

OKEMOS

Meridian Historical Village

5113 Marsh Road, Okemos, MI 48805 (42.728011, -84.413941)

(517) 347-7300, meridianhistoricalvillage@gmail.com, www.meridianhistoricalvillage.org
Hours: May-Oct: Sat 10am-2pm. *Admission:* Free. *Site Info:* Free on-site parking. Not wheelchair accessible. Tour guide available; check in at general store.

The 19th-century Meridian Historical Village is a living history museum with nine historic structures.

OVID

Mary Myers Museum

131 E. Williams, Ovid, MI 48866 (43.006622, -84.371050)
(989) 834-5421, ovidhs67@yahoo.com,
www.ovidhistoricalsociety.weebly.com
Hours: 2nd and 4th Sun monthly 2-4pm. Also by appointment.
Admission: Donations accepted. *Site Info:* Street parking.

The Ovid Historical Society maintains the Mary Myers Museum, an 1869 Italianate style furnished for this period.

OWOSSO

Steam Railroading Institute

405 S. Washington St., Owosso, MI 48867 (42.994336, -84.170592)
(989) 725-9464, terry.b@mstrp.com, www.michigansteamtrain.com
Hours: Summer: Wed-Sun 10am-5pm; Winter: Fri-Sun 10am-4pm.
Admission: $5. Excursion prices vary. *Site Info:* On-site parking. Partially wheelchair accessible; visitors center and some backshop area. Tour guide available on weekends; price included in admission.

The Steam Railroading Institute educates the public about steam-era railroad technology and its impact on the culture and economy of the Great Lakes region by safely operating, preserving, exhibiting, and interpreting historic railroad equipment. Operated by the Michigan State Trust for Railway Preservation, the institute offers several steam and diesel excursions throughout the year. Its museum features interactive steam-era educational programs.

Shiawassee County Historical Society Archives and Museum

1997 N. M-52, Owosso, MI 48867 (43.026379, -84.176892)
(989) 723-2371, archer@charter.net,
www.shiawasseecountyhistsoc.org
Hours: Apr-Sep: Sun 1-4pm. Also by appointment. *Admission:* Donations accepted. *Site Info:* Free on-site and street parking. Wheelchair accessible. Tour guide available.

The Shiawassee County Historical Society Archives and Museum collects and displays items pertaining to Shiawassee County, especially family histories and the beginning of Shiawassee County.

REMUS

Remus Area Historical Museum
324 S. Sheridan Ave., Remus, MI 49340 (43.594499, -85.145384)
(989) 967-8153, museum@winntel.net, www.remus.org
Hours: 11am-3pm. *Admission:* Free. *Site Info:* Free on-site parking.
Wheelchair accessible. Self-guided.

The Remus Area Historical Society preserves the rich heritage of the
Remus area by acquiring historical artifacts and genealogy records
of local families.

SAGINAW

Castle Museum of Saginaw County History
500 Federal Ave., Saginaw, MI 48607 (43.431247, -83.935611)
(989) 752-2861, ksanta@castlemuseum.org, www.castlemuseum.org
Hours: Tue-Sat 10am-4:30pm, Sun 1-4:30pm. *Admission:* Adults
$1, Youth $0.50. *Site Info:* Free on-site and street parking.
Wheelchair accessible. Guided tours by reservation; $2/person.

Housed in Saginaw's original post office, the Castle Museum of
Saginaw County History offers three floors of exhibits exploring
Saginaw County's rich history. Permanent exhibits include
archaeology, lumbering, manufacturing, and the postal service. The
museum is also home to one of the region's largest working model
trains, which has more than 1,000 feet of track.

Saginaw Railway Museum
900 Maple St., Saginaw, MI 48602 (43.407499, -83.98459)
(989) 790-7994, info@saginawrailwaymuseum.org,
www.saginawrailwaymuseum.org
Hours: Apr-Nov: 1st & 3rd Sat 1-4pm. Closed holiday weekends.
Admission: Donations accepted. $20 donations receive a one-year,
individual membership. *Site Info:* Free on-site parking. Partially
wheelchair accessible. Self-guided.

The Saginaw Railway Museum is located in a restored 1907 Pere
Marquette depot that once stood in Hemlock, Michigan. Exhibits
include the Mershon switch tower, which operated until 1987 in
nearby Carrollton; a former U.S. Navy switch engine; a C&O
combine car that houses the Etter Collection; a static Alco
locomotive; and two cabooses. There is also a large HO Scale
railroad layout, loosely based on the region in the 1950s.

Theodore Roethke Home Museum
1805 Gratiot Avenue, Saginaw, MI 48602 (43.414834, -83.987305)
(989) 928-0430, info@roethkehouse.org, www.roethkehouse.org

Hours: By appointment. *Admission:* $5. *Site Info:* Street parking. Not wheelchair accessible. Tour guide available by appointment.

The Friends of Theodore Roethke Foundation promote, preserve, and protect the literary legacy of Pulitzer Prize-winning poet Theodore Roethke by restoring his family residence in Saginaw for cultural and educational opportunities. Roethke's childhood home has a Michigan Historical Marker, National Literary Landmark designation, and is in the National Register of Historic Places.

SANFORD

Sanford Centennial Museum

2222 Smith St., Sanford, MI 48657 (43.676264, -84.388909)
(989) 687-9048, logmarks@tds.net, www.sanfordhist.org
Hours: Memorial Day to Labor Day: Sat 10am-5pm, Sun 1-5pm. Also by appointment. *Admission:* Free. *Site Info:* Free on-site parking. Wheelchair accessible. Self-guided.

The Sanford Centennial Museum includes eight restored and furnished historic buildings—two schools, a general store, a log cabin, a township hall, a church, an implement barn, and a train depot. Inside these buildings are vintage tools, implements from the logging days, political memorabilia, dentist's office, barbershop, doctor's office, and more. Highlights include a train engine, boxcar, two cabooses, and Michigan logging wheels.

SHEPHERD

Little Red Schoolhouse Museum

306 Chippewa St., Shepherd, MI 48883 (43.521430, -84.687026)
(989) 772-0718, calauffer@charter.net, www.shepherdahs.org
Hours: During Maple Syrup Festival. Also by appointment. *Admission:* Donations accepted. *Site Info:* Parking on school campus. Not wheelchair accessible. Tour guide available by appointment; call Patti Sandel at (989) 828-5534 or Joyce Noyes at (989) 828-5319.

The Little Red Schoolhouse Museum is located in a late 1800s one-room school. It features school artifacts from the early 1900s and composite photos of graduates of the Shepherd Public Schools system.

Shepherd Powerhouse Museum

314 W. Maple St., Shepherd, MI 48883 (43.523331, -84.695148)
(989) 772-0718, calauffer@charter.net, www.shepherdahs.org
Hours: During Maple Syrup Festival and Ice Cream Social. Also by appointment. *Admission:* Donations accepted. *Site Info:* Free

parking by museum. Not wheelchair accessible. Tour guide available by appointment; call Larry Noyes at (989) 828-5319.

Located in the former Shepherd Powerhouse, this museum offers a glimpse into Shepherd area history. On display are artifacts from the area, family records, scrapbooks, and memorabilia.

ST. JOHNS

Paine-Gillam-Scott Museum

106 Maple St., St. Johns, MI 48879 (43.0013461, -84.559155)
(989) 224-2894, pgsmuseum@hotmail.com, www.pgsmuseum.com
Hours: May-Dec: Sun 1-4pm and Wed 2-7pm. *Admission:* Adult $2, Family $5. *Site Info:* Free street parking. Not wheelchair accessible. Tour guide available.

The Paine-Gillam-Scott Museum, located in a furnished house built in 1860, is reflective of Clinton County's history. The carriage house has agricultural and industrial displays. There is also a doctor's office, dentist's office with driver's quarters, and a general store.

ST. LOUIS

St. Louis Historic Park

110 E. Crawford St., St. Louis, MI 48880 (43.405394, -84.606985)
(989) 681-3017, stlouisdda@stlouismi.com,
www.stlouismi.com/1/stlouis/Historical_Society.asp
Hours: Thu 1-4pm. *Admission: Site Info:* Free on-site parking. Wheelchair accessible. Tour guide available by appointment.

The St. Louis Area Historical Society's museum is located in in the restored Pere Marquette train depot at the St. Louis Historic Park. Also at the park is the Transportation Pavilion—which includes a 1917 Republic Truck, Indian dugout canoe, and other transportation items—and a restored wooden toll booth from M-46 Plank Road. The society is currently restoring a log cabin and two-story house.

SUNFIELD

Welch Museum

161 Main St., Sunfield, MI 48890 (42.762407, -84.993416)
sunfieldhistoricalsociety@gmail.com,
www.sunfieldhistoricalsociety.com
Hours: Apr-Dec: Mon 10am-2pm, Wed 2-6pm, and Sat 10am-2pm. Closed holidays, *Admission:* Free. *Site Info:* Street parking. Wheelchair accessible. Tour guide available.

Operated by the Sunfield Historical Society, the Welch Museum features a turn-of-the-century classroom, hands-on displays, and photos of students who graduated from Sunfield High School (1914-1963). Built within the museum is a fully furnished 1860 log cabin.

UNION CITY

Hammond House Museum
210 Charlotte St., Union City, MI 49094 (42.068059, -85.136959)
(517) 741-7733, uchistoricalsociety@yahoo.com,
Hours: Open for special events and by appointment. *Admission:* Adults (12+) $2.

The Hammond House Museum is located in an 1840s Greek Revival house and features an attached display area.

EASTERN

ADRIAN

Adrian Dominican Sisters' Madden Hall
1257 E. Siena Heights Drive, Adrian, MI 49221 (41.906653, -84.014447)
(517) 266-3580, nfoley@adriandominicans.org, www.adriandominicans.org
Hours: Mon-Fri 9am-5pm. Also by appointment. *Admission:* Free.
Site Info: Parking across the street. Wheelchair accessible. Tour guide available upon request.

Located at the main campus of the Adrian Dominican Sisters, Madden Hall houses a historical display that is organized into three time periods: 1879 to 1933, 1933 to 1962, and 1963 to present. Each contains narrative panels, photos, documents, and artifacts of its respective period. Also located within Madden Hall is the Historic Holy Rosary Chapel, which was built in 1905-1907.

Lenawee County Historical Museum
110 E. Church St., Adrian, MI 49221 (41.897448, -84.037320)
(517) 265-6071, lenaweemuseum@yahoo.com,
freepages.history.rootsweb.ancestry.com/~keller/museum/work
Hours: Tue-Fri 10am-2pm, Sat 10am-4pm. *Admission:* Free. *Site Info:* Free on-site parking. Wheelchair accessible. Tour guide available; group tours by appointment.

Exhibits in the Lenawee County Historical Museum feature the history of Lenawee County, its pioneers, railroads, and industries. The 100-year-old building is listed in the National Register of Historical Places and also includes an auditorium and a large archive of genealogical information.

ALGONAC

Algonac-Clay Township Museum
1240 St. Clair River Drive, Algonac, MI 48001 (42.619159, -82.530252)
(810) 794-9015, achs@algonac-clay-history.com,
www.achistory.com
Hours: Mar-Dec: Sat-Sun 1-4pm, Wed 6-8pm. Also by appointment. *Admission:* Donations accepted. *Site Info:* Free on-site parking. Wheelchair accessible. Tour guide available.

The Algonac-Clay Township Museum has exhibits pertaining to the area's Native American tribes, the military, freighters, and Tall Ship memorabilia. There is also an exhibit that changes on a yearly basis.

Algonac-Clay Maritime Museum
1117 St. Clair River Drive, Algonac, MI 48001 (42.6187171, -82.5308297)
(810) 794-9015, achs@algonac-clay-history.com,
www.achistory.com
Hours: Call for hours. *Site Info:* Free on-site parking. Wheelchair accessible. Tour guide available.

The Maritime Museum features boating artifacts and shares the history of boating.

ANN ARBOR

Bentley Historical Library
University of Michigan, 1150 Beal Ave., Ann Arbor, MI 48109 (42.290879, -83.713561)
(734) 764-3482, kljania@umich.edu, www.bentley.umich.edu
Hours: Mon-Fri 9am-5pm. *Admission:* Free. *Site Info:* Free on-site parking. Wheelchair accessible.

Established in 1935, the Bentley Historical Library has amassed extensive holdings on the history of the state and the university. Attractions include an exhibit in the reading room and "Tappan's Vision" in the Whiting Room. (Henry Tappan was president of the school in the mid 1800s.)

Detroit Observatory

1398 E. Ann, Ann Arbor, MI 48109 (42.281928, -83.731618)
(734) 764-3482, kljania@umich.edu,
www.bentley.umich.edu/observatory
Hours: See website or call ahead. *Admission:* Donations accepted. *Site Info:* Metered street parking. Not wheelchair accessible. Tour guide available.

Managed by the Bentley Historical Library, the Detroit Observatory stands essentially as it did in 1854. The original astronomical instruments—including the 6-inch Pistor & Martins meridian circle and the 12 5/8-inch Henry Fitz, Jr. refracting telescopes—remain intact and operational. The dome is turned manually by pulling a continuous rope.

Gerald R. Ford Presidential Library

National Archives Records Administration, 1000 Beal Ave., Ann Arbor, MI 48109 (42.288193, -83.712927)
(734) 205-0555, ford.library@nara.gov,
www.fordlibrarymuseum.gov
Hours: Mon-Fri 8:45am-4:45pm. *Admission:* Free. *Site Info:* Free on-site parking. Wheelchair accessible.

The Gerald R. Ford Presidential Library preserves the written record and physical history of presidents while providing special programs and exhibits that serve the community. Located on the campus of the University of Michigan, the library offers small-scale, temporary exhibits.

Kempf House Museum

312 S. Division St., Ann Arbor, MI 48104 (42.278963, -83.744384)
(734) 994-4898, kempfhousemuseum@gmail.com,
www.kempfhousemuseum.org
Hours: Spring and Fall: Sun 1-4pm. Also by appointment.
Admission: Donations accepted. *Site Info:* Street and public parking. Wheelchair accessible. Tour guide available.

The 1853 Greek Revival Kempf House interprets Ann Arbor history and Victorian lifestyles from 1850 to 1910.

Michigan Theater

603 E. Liberty St., Ann Arbor, MI 48104 (42.279704, -83.742019)
(734) 668-8397, info@michtheater.org, www.michtheater.org
Hours: Mon-Sat 3-10pm, Sun 3-9pm. *Admission:* $7-$10 for films.

Site Info: Metered street parking; nearby parking structures include Maynard and Liberty Square. Wheelchair accessible. Tour guide available by appointment.

The historic Michigan Theater showcases fine films 365 days a year. The Ford Gallery highlights the founding of Ann Arbor, the building of the Michigan Theater, the restoration of the theater, and the individuals who have been pivotal in the theater's history.

Museum on Main Street

500 N. Main St., Ann Arbor, MI 48106 (42.285161, -83.7480261)
(734) 662-9092, wchs-500@ameritech.net,
www.washtenawhistory.org
Hours: Sat-Sun 12-4pm. *Admission:* Donations accepted. *Site Info:* Free on-site parking. Wheelchair accessible. Tour guide available.

Located at the corner of East Kingsley and Beakes streets, the Museum on Main Street considers different aspects of Washtenaw County's history.

Sutherland-Wilson Farm Museum

797 Textile Road, Ann Arbor, MI 48108 (42.199163, -83.740661)
(734) 971-2384, donbet@comcast.net, www.pittsfieldhistory.org
Hours: By appointment. *Admission:* Free. *Site Info:* Free on-site parking. Wheelchair accessible. Tour guide available by appointment.

Maintained by the Pittsfield Township Historical Society, the Sutherland-Wilson Farm Museum is located in an 1830s Greek Revival home and features furniture from the 1830s to 1900s. Outbuildings include a barn, carriage house, ice house, wood shed, and pump house. These buildings feature a wagon, carriage, farm equipment, tools, etc.

William L. Clements Library

University of Michigan, 909 S. University Ave., Ann Arbor, MI 48109 (42.275262, -83.737994)
(734) 764-2347, www.clements.umich.edu

The William L. Clements Library features changing exhibits—focusing on different aspects of collections that would interest both an expert bibliophile and the casual reader—in its front hall.

NOTE: The library is undergoing renovation through Fall 2015 and does not have exhibit space in its temporary location (580 Ellsworth Road, Ann Arbor). The library plans to resume on-site exhibits after moving back to its home location.

BAD AXE

Huron County Historical Society

Multiple locations; see website.
(989) 712-0050, huroncountyhistoricalsociety@yahoo.com,
www.thehchs.org

The Huron County Historical Society consists of 11 historical
society chapters located in Huron County. Each year, the society
hosts a countywide museum weekend, scheduled the last full
weekend of September. Most of the county's museums will be open
with different displays and activities from 11am-4pm both days. See
website for more information.

BELLEVILLE

Belleville Area Museum and Archives

405 Main St., Belleville, MI 48111 (42.208364, -83.490912)
(734) 697-1944, kdallos@provide.net, Find on Facebook
Hours: Fall/Winter: Tue 3-7pm, Wed-Sat 12-4pm; Spring/Summer:
Mon 12-4pm, Tue 3-7pm, Wed-Fri 12-4pm. *Admission:* $2. *Site
Info:* On-site and street parking. Wheelchair accessible. Self-guided;
group bookings call ahead.

Located in the 1875 Van Buren Township Hall, the Belleville Area
Museum and Archives highlights the history of Belleville as well as
Van Buren and Sumpter townships.

Yankee Air Museum

47884 D St., Belleville, MI 48111 (42.238860, -83.508667)
(734) 483-4030, supportyankee@yankeeairmuseum.org,
www.yankeeairmuseum.org
Hours: Tue-Sat 10am-4pm. *Admission:* Adults $5, Students $5,
Family (two adults and two children) $8, Children (0-17) free. *Site
Info:* Free on-site parking. Wheelchair accessible. Tour guide
available by appointment; call (734) 483-4030.

The Yankee Air Museum challenges, educates, and inspires visitors
to embrace aviation's past as a vehicle to the future. Static aircraft
displays include an F-4 Phantom II, U-H1 "Huey" Helicopter, RF-
86, F-86, F101 Voodoo, and more. Exhibits center on the Willow
Run Bomber Plant and its contributions during WWII, as well as
more current global conflicts.

BERKLEY

Berkley Historical Museum

3338 Coolidge Hwy, Berkley, MI 48072 (42.502504, -83.183545)

(248) 658-3335, museum@berkleymich.net,
www.berkleymich.org/community_museum.shtm

Located in the former fire hall at City Hall, the Berkley Historical Museum displays memorabilia from the city's archives and items contributed by local residents. Every year at Christmas, the museum features a holiday-themed display.
*Information may not be current.

BIRMINGHAM

Birmingham Historical Museum & Park

556 W. Maple, Birmingham, MI 48009 (42.546907, -83.220241)
(248) 530-1928, museum@bhamgov.org,
www.bhamgov.org/museum
Hours: Wed-Sat 1-4pm. Also by appointment. *Admission:* Adults $5, Seniors and Students $3, Children (0-4) free. Admission includes tours of the Allen and Hunter houses. *Site Info:* Two hours free parking at nearby Chester Street Structure. Wheelchair accessible. Tour guide available.

The Birmingham Historical Museum & Park focuses on Birmingham/Bloomfield Township area history. The four-acre park features two historic buildings. The 1822 John West Hunter House is the oldest house in Birmingham and is interpreted as a pioneer-era, 19th-century dwelling with period furnishings. The 1928 Allen House features changing exhibits that focus on local history, permanent exhibits pertaining to the 1920s, and a Flint Faience tile fireplace from a local elementary school.

BLOOMFIELD HILLS

Cranbrook Archives

39221 Woodward Ave Bloomfield Hills, MI 48303 (42.568934, -83.249870)
(248) 645-3583, www.cranbrook.edu/archives
Hours: Mon-Fri 8:30am-4:30pm. Closed major holidays. *Site Info:* Wheelchair accessible. Free on-site parking.

The Cranbrook Archives serves as the research center for study of Cranbrook's heritage in the fields of education, science, art, architecture, and design. The facility hosts rotating exhibits in its "From the Archives" series, which highlights different materials from its collections.
*Information may not be current.

BRIDGEPORT

Bridgeport Historic Village & Museum
6190 Dixie Hwy, Bridgeport, MI 48722 (43.357268, -83.880183)
(989) 777-5230, damccartney2@yahoo.com,
www.bridgeporthistorical.blogspot.com
Hours: Tue-Sat 1-5pm. *Admission:* Free. *Site Info:* Free on-site
parking. Wheelchair accessible. Tour guide available; larger groups
cost $2/person and should schedule in advance. Bridgefest (Jun),
Flea and Farm Market (Jun-Sep), Concerts in the Park (Jun-Aug),
Pioneer Christmas (Dec).

The Bridgeport Historic Village includes seven different buildings,
including an 1850s Greek Revival home, an 19th-century one-room
school house, a replica of the area's 1941 fire department, and more.
Highlights include a 1912 Model T Ford, windmill, etc.

BRIGHTON

1885 Lyon One-Room Schoolhouse Museum
14455 Buno Road, Brighton, MI 48114 (42.454860, -83.653971)
(810) 250-7276, info@brightonareahistorical.com,
www.brightonareahistorical.com
Hours: Thu 9am-12pm; 3rd Sun monthly 1-4pm. *Admission:* Free.
Site Info: On-site parking. Wheelchair accessible. Tour guide
available by appointment.

Operated by the Brighton Area Historical Society, the 1885 Lyon
School is a fully restored one-room schoolhouse set in 1900. It
features classic maple/cast iron student desks with inkwells. A small
museum highlights local memorabilia, including early veterinarian
tools and photos of Brighton.

City of Brighton Arts, Culture and History (COBACH) Center
202 W. Main St. Brighton, MI 48114 (42.529658, -83.781850)
(810) 229-2784, info@brightonareahistorical.com,
www.brightonareahistorical.com
Hours: Sun-Fri 5pm-8pm, Sat 9am-12pm. *Admission:* Free. *Site
Info:* Free street and off-street parking. Wheelchair accessible.

Located in a former 1879 firehouse, the COBACH Center is
operated by three local nonprofits, including the Brighton Area
Historical Society. The historical society changes its displays in the
center every six to eight weeks.

CANTON

Bartlett/Travis House at Preservation Park
500 N. Ridge Road, Canton, MI 48187 (42.308680, -83.534621)

(734) 495-0274, cantonhist@comcast.net,
www.cantonhistoricalsociety.org
Hours: Mid-May to Mid-Oct: Sun 9am-1pm. *Admission:* Free. *Site Info:* Free on-site parking. Partially wheelchair accessible. Call ahead for tour guide availability.

Operated by the Canton Historical Society, the Bartlett/Travis House at Preservation Park is a Victorian-style house that was built in the 1860s and "Victorianized" about 1900. There is also a barn full of old farm equipment. (The society's main museum, a one-room schoolhouse located on Canton Center Road, is closed for repairs and restoration. Call ahead for its reopening date).

CAPAC

Capac Community Historical Museum
401 E. Kempf Court, Capac, MI 48014 (43.016956, -82.923892)
(810) 395-2859, capacmuseum@hotmail.com,
http://capachistoricalsocietymuseum.wordpress.com
Hours: Mon-Fri 11am-3pm, Sun 1-4pm. *Admission:* Donations accepted. *Site Info:* Free on-site parking. Wheelchair accessible. Tour guide available.

The Capac Community Historical Museum maintains a museum in the restored Grand Trunk Western depot, which features exhibits relating to Capac and the Thumb area. On display is the Kempf Model City (a mechanical city, 40 feet long and four feet wide). Also on site is a Grand Truck Western caboose—which includes several railroad artifacts—and the Kempf Historical Museum, which features area artifacts, postcards, and a historical research library.

CASEVILLE

Maccabees Hall Museum
6733 Prospect St., Caseville, MI 48725 (43.942544, -83.271314)
(989) 856-9090, chscm@comcast.net, www.thehchs.org/caseville
Hours: Wed-Sat 12-4:30pm. *Admission:* Free. *Site Info:* Free on-site parking. Wheelchair accessible. Tour guide available.

The Historical Society of Caseville maintains a museum in the 1890s Maccabees Hall. Displays include fishing, farming, lumbering, school, and household objects.

CHESTERFIELD

Chesterfield Historical Village
47275 Sugarbush Road, Chesterfield, MI 48047 (42.650358, -82.823426)

(586) 749-3713, royfrivard@yahoo.com,
www.chesterfieldhistoricalsociety.org
Hours: Open for regularly scheduled events and by appointment.
Admission: Free. During special events, the suggested donation is
$1/adult and $2/family. *Site Info:* Free on-site and street parking.
Wheelchair accessible.

The Chesterfield Historical Society collects, safeguards, stores, and
displays the history of Chesterfield. The Chesterfield Historical
Village includes four buildings: a one-room schoolhouse (used from
1862 to 1954) and outhouse, a log cabin with a springhouse and
spiral outhouse, a cobbler shop, and a working blacksmith shop.

CLARKSTON

Clarkston Heritage Museum
6495 Clarkston Road, Clarkston, MI 48346 (42.739264,
-83.408611)
(248) 922-0270, info@clarkstonhistorical.org,
www.clarkstonhistorical.org
Hours: Mon-Wed 10am-9pm, Thu-Sat 10am-6pm. *Admission:* Free.
Site Info: Free on-site parking. Wheelchair accessible. Self-guided.

Located in the Independence Township Library, the Clarkston
Heritage Museum offers displays that focus on Clarkston history.
Exhibits change approximately twice a year and have covered
everything from local farms to the area's long-standing tradition of
4th of July parades.

CLAWSON

Clawson Historical Museum
41 Fisher Court, Clawson, MI 48017 (42.536712, -83.145627)
(248) 588-9169, historicalmuseum@cityofclawson.com,
www.clawsonhistoricalsociety.org
Hours: Sun and Wed 1-4pm. *Admission:* Free. *Site Info:* Not
wheelchair accessible. Free parking.

The Clawson Historical Museum preserves and promotes the history
of Clawson and the surrounding areas. The museum building is a
three-story house built by Oswald and Deborah Fischer in the 1920s.
It features 11 rooms furnished to reflect that era.

CLAY TOWNSHIP

Log Cabin and Detroit Urban Railway Wait Station and Annex
4710 Point Tremble Road, Clay Township, MI 48001 (42.622376,
-82.572234)

(810) 794-9015, achs@algonac-clay-history.com,
www.achistory.com
Hours: Open Michigan Log Cabin Day. *Admission:* Donations accepted. *Site Info:* Free on-site parking. Wheelchair accessible. Tour guide available.

Maintained by the Clay Township Historical Society, the log cabin dates back to the late 1880s. Next to the cabin is a section of the interurban railway track and the original interurban waiting station that served Pearl Beach from approximately 1892 until the 1930s.

CLINTON

Southern Michigan Railroad Society

320 S. Division St., Clinton, MI 49236 (42.071001, -83.974164)
(517) 456-7677, cyngiven@gmail.com,
www.southernmichiganrailroad.com
Hours: Museum open during scheduled train excursions or by appointment. *Admission:* Train fares vary; museum admission is free. *Site Info:* Free on-site and street parking. Not wheelchair accessible. Self-guided.

The Southern Michigan Railroad Society offers excursions on one of the first railroad branch lines in Michigan—a rail corridor that connected the Michigan Southern line with the Michigan Central line in Jackson. See website for schedule and boarding locations. The organization also operates a railroading museum at its Clinton Boarding Station. Attractions include a 1943 General Electric 44-ton locomotive #75 (former Western Maryland), 1957 New York New Haven cupola caboose, and more.

CLINTON TOWNSHIP

Clinton Township Historical Village

40700 Romeo Plank Road, Clinton Township, MI 48038 (42.594979, -82.928882)
(586) 263-9173, jphungerford@gmail.com, www.ctwphc.org
Hours: Call or check website for hours. *Admission:* Free. *Site Info:* Free parking. Wheelchair accessible. Tour guide available.

The Clinton Township Historical Commission is responsible for the general administration of the township's historical properties, including the buildings in Clinton Township Historical Village. **Information may not be current.*

Lorenzo Cultural Center

Building K, Macomb Community College, 44575 Garfield, Clinton Township, MI 48038 (42.617481, -82.95707)
(586) 445-7348, culturalcenter@macomb.edu,
www.lorenzoculturalcenter.com

Hours: Wed-Sat 10am-4pm, Sun 1-4pm. *Admission:* Free. *Site Info:* Free on-site parking. Wheelchair accessible. Contact the center at least two weeks in advance to schedule a guided tour. See website.

Each year, the Lorenzo Cultural Center presents a themed anchor program and numerous presentations that explore the influences and experiences that shape the community's heritage, examine topics from a variety of perspectives, and create interactive opportunities for learning, celebration, and entertainment.

COLUMBIAVILLE

Columbiaville Historical Society Museum
4718 First St., Columbiaville, MI 48619 (43.157170, -83.410991)
(810) 793-2932, cville.historical.society.2@gmail.com,
www.columbiavillehistoricalsociety.blogspot.com
Hours: May-Oct: 1st and 3rd Fri monthly 1-4pm. Also by appointment. *Admission:* Donations accepted. *Site Info:* Free on-site parking. Wheelchair accessible. Tour guide available.

Attractions at the Columbiaville Historical Society Museum include Native American arrowheads, mounted birds, quilts, furniture, books, photographs, and antique household and farm implements.

DAVISON

Davison Area Historical Museum
Woolley Veterinarian Building
263 E. Fourth St., Davison, MI 48423 (43.033845, -83.515433)
(810) 658-2286, info@davisonmuseum.org,
www.davisonmuseum.org
Hours: Thu 10am-2pm. *Admission:* Donations accepted. *Site Info:* Free on-site parking. Partially wheelchair accessible. Tour guide available.

The Davison Area Historical Museum features everyday artifacts from the mid-1800s to 1940. Exhibits include a 1900 kitchen, dry goods store, millinery shop, and Davison's first "post office." Next to the museum is the Woolley Veterinarian Building, which visitors may access only when accompanied by a docent. The former office of Dr. Floyd E. Woolley displays all its original medicines, equipment, and other artifacts.

Kitchen School
Southwest Corner of M-15 (State Road) and Bristol Road, Davison, MI 48423 (42.976557, -83.507045)
(810) 658-2286, info@davisonmuseum.org,
www.davisonmuseum.org
Hours: By appointment. *Admission:* Free. *Site Info:* Free on-site

parking. Building is wheelchair accessible but grounds are unpaved. Tour guide available.

Dating back to the late 1800s, Kitchen School was named for Silas Kitchen—one of the area's homesteaders. The building is restored to its 1940s appearance and includes an outhouse, wood stove, and child-powered merry-go-round.

DEARBORN

1833 Commandant's Quarters
21950 Michigan Ave., Dearborn, MI 48124 (42.306683, -83.243872)
(313) 565-3000, jtate@ci.dearborn.mi.us,
www.dearbornhistoricalmuseum.com
Hours: By appointment. *Admission:* Donations accepted. *Site Info:* On-site and street parking available for a fee. Not wheelchair accessible. Tour guide available by appointment.

Part of the Detroit Arsenal, this structure served as home to 19 different commandants and their families from 1833 to 1875. The current portion of the arsenal wall and entrance gate are replicas. Today, the building is listed in the National Register of Historic Places and features rooms decorated in the style of the era from 1833-1875.

Arab American National Museum
13624 Michigan Ave., Dearborn, MI 48126 (42.322125, -83.176617)
(313) 582-2266, ksilarski@accesscommunity.org,
www.arabamericanmuseum.org
Hours: Wed-Sat 10am-6pm, Sun 12-5pm. *Admission:* Adults $8, Students & Seniors $4, Children (0-5) free. *Site Info:* Free parking in city lot north of museum. Wheelchair accessible. Group tours available for 8+ people; cost is $10/adults, $5/seniors, and $5/students.

The Arab American National Museum is the first and only museum in the world devoted to the history, culture, and contributions of Arab Americans. Interactive exhibits discuss Arab immigration to the U.S., Arab American lifestyles and traditions, and famous Arab Americans. Two rotating galleries feature traditional and contemporary art, history, and culture.

Automotive Hall of Fame
21400 Oakwood Blvd., Dearborn, MI 48124 (42.301880, -83.237400)
(313) 240-4000, AHOF@thedrivingspirit.org,
www.automotivehalloffame.org
Hours: Wed-Sun 9am-5pm. Closed some holidays. *Admission:*

Adults $8, Seniors $6, Students $6, Youth (5-18) $4. Tour groups of 15+ are $4/person. *Site Info:* Private parking lot. Wheelchair accessible. Tour guides available, no extra cost.

The Automotive Hall of Fame recognizes outstanding achievement in automotive-related industries and preserves automotive heritage through visual and interactive exhibits, automobiles, and authentic artifacts.

Dearborn Historical Museum
1831 Richard Gardner House

915 S. Brady, Dearborn, MI 48124 (42.308073, -83.240420)
(313) 565-3000, jtate@ci.dearborn.mi.us,
www.dearbornhistoricalmuseum.com
Hours: Tue-Fri 9am-4pm. *Admission:* Donations accepted. *Site Info:* Free on-site and street parking. Not wheelchair accessible. Tour guide available by appointment.

The Dearborn Historical Museum is based out of two buildings from the old Dearbornville Arsenal: the McFadden-Ross House (previously the Powder Magazine) and the 1833 Commandant's Quarters (listed on the previous page). The McFadden-Ross House features exhibits about Dearborn's brick manufacturers and pioneer living, complete with a one-room classroom. Also on site is the 1831 Richard Gardner House, the oldest home in Dearborn, which is open only by appointment. The museum also provides tour brochures of the greater Dearborn area.

The Henry Ford

20900 Oakwood Blvd., Dearborn, MI 48124 (42.303108, -83.233108)
(800) 835-5237, bfrcsubscriptions@thehenryford.org,
www.thehenryford.org
Site Info: On-site parking; $5/vehicle except for members.

Henry Ford Museum

Hours: Daily 9:30am-5pm. Closed Thanksgiving and Christmas Day. *Admission:* Adults $17, Seniors (62+) $15, Youth (5-12) $12.50, Children (0-4) free. *Site Info:* On-site parking; $5/vehicle except for members. Wheelchair accessible.

The Henry Ford Museum's exhibits highlight the innovators who made America a manufacturing superpower, the evolution of American freedom, early aviation pioneers, automotive influence on American culture, a collection of vehicles that once transported former presidents, the Dymaxion House, and more.

Greenfield Village

Hours: Mid-Apr to Nov 3: Daily 9:30am-5pm; Nov 8 to
Dec 1: Fri-Sun: 9:30am-5pm; Dec 2-31: Closed except for
Holiday Nights in Greenfield Village. *Admission:* Adults
$24, Seniors (62+) $22, Youth (5-12) $17.50, Children (0-
4) free. *Site Info:* On-site parking; $5/vehicle except for
members. Partially wheelchair accessible.

Greenfield Village includes 83 authentic, historic
structures including Noah Webster's home, where he
wrote the first American dictionary; Thomas Edison's
Menlo Park laboratory; and the courthouse where
Abraham Lincoln practiced law. Visitors can ride in a
genuine Model T, "pull" glass with world-class artisans,
watch 1867 baseball, or ride a train with a 19th-century
steam engine.

Ford Rouge Factory Tour

www.thehenryford.org/rouge
Hours: See website. *Admission:* Adults $15, Youth $11,
Seniors $14, Children (0-2) free.
Tours begin at the Henry Ford Museum with buses
departing every 20 minutes from 9:20am-3pm. The self-
guided tour includes a film detailing the history of the
Rouge, a multi-sensory theater experience looking at how
automobiles are made, a tour of the assembly plant where
the new Ford F-150s are made, and more.

DETROIT

Charles H. Wright Museum of African American History

315 E. Warren Ave., Detroit, MI 48201 (42.358370, -83.060889)
(313) 494-5800, ted@chwmuseum.org, www.thewright.org
Hours: Tue-Sat 9am-5pm, Sun 1-5pm. Closed Mon, except for
MLK Day and during Black History Month. *Admission:* Adults (13-
61) $8, Seniors (62+) $5, Youth (3-12) $5, Members and children
(0-2) free. *Site Info:* Free and metered street parking. On-site
parking (entrance at John R. Street); cost is $5 before 4pm and $3
afterward. Wheelchair accessible. Tour guide available by
appointment; call (313) 494-5808 or e-mail *tours@chwmuseum.org*.

Founded in 1965, the Charles H. Wright Museum of African
American History is the world's largest institution dedicated to the
African American experience. This 125,000-square-foot museum
includes "And Still We Rise: Our Journey Through African
American History and Culture," an interactive exhibit that contains
more than 20 galleries traveling over time and across geographic
boundaries.

Detroit Historical Museum

5401 Woodward Ave., Detroit, MI 48202 (42.359735, -83.066812)
(313) 833-7935, www.detroithistorical.org
Hours: Tue-Fri 9:30am-4pm, Sat 10am-5pm, Sun 12-5pm.
Admission: Free. *Site Info:* On-site parking; $5/car. Wheelchair
accessible. Tour guide available by appointment. (Dec).

The Detroit Historical Museum's exhibits consider the relationship
between the city and the automotive industry, its early history from
1701-1901, its role as the "Arsenal of Democracy," and more.

Detroit Public Library's Burton Historical Collection

5201 Woodward Ave., Detroit, MI 48202 (42.3584249, -83.066566)
(313) 481-1401, bhc@detroitpubliclibrary.org,
www.detroitpubliclibrary.org
Hours: Tue-Wed 12-8pm, Thu-Sat 10am-6pm. *Admission:* Free. *Site*
Info: Metered street parking. Wheelchair accessible.

The Burton Historical Collection began as the private collection of
Detroit attorney Clarence M. Burton. Located on the first floor of
the Detroit Public Library, the collection built upon its foundation of
Detroit history to also include the history of the Old Northwest, New
France, and Canada. The Detroit Public Library is also home to
history exhibits that include items from sportscaster Ernie Harwell's
baseball collection and more.

Dossin Great Lakes Museum

100 Strand Drive, Belle Isle Detroit, MI 48207 (42.334477,
-82.985393)
(313) 833-5538, www.detroithistorical.org
Hours: Sat and Sun 11am-4 pm. *Admission:* Free. *Site Info:*
Wheelchair accessible.

Located on Belle Isle, the Dossin Great Lakes Museum is dedicated
to showcasing the story of the Great Lakes, with a special emphasis
on Detroit's role in regional and national maritime history.

Ford Piquette Avenue Plant

461 PiquetteAve., Detroit, MI 48202 (42.368585, -83.065149)
(313) 872-8759, www.tplex.org
Hours: Apr-Oct: Wed-Fri 10am-4pm, Sat 9am-4pm, Sun 12-4pm.
Admission: Adults $10, Seniors (65+) $8, Students (with school ID)
$5. *Site Info:* Free parking. Wheelchair accessible. Tour guide
available.

The Model T Automotive Heritage Complex, Inc. (T-PLEX) is
dedicated to the preservation of the 1904 Piquette Avenue Plant, the
first factory owned/built by Ford Motor Company (1904-1910) and
the birthplace of the Model T Ford. Changing exhibits and vintage
vehicles tell the story of Ford Motor Company during the Piquette

era. This National Historic Landmark is also listed in State Register of Historic Sites.

Hellenic Museum of Michigan

67 E. Kirby, Detroit, MI 48202 (42.360774, -83.06535)
(313) 831-6100, sam@zacharydetroit.com, www.hellenicmi.org
Site Info: Metered street parking. Wheelchair accessible. Self-guided.

The Hellenic Museum of Michigan features artifacts and photographs of Greek immigrants and Greek Americans.

Historic Fort Wayne

6325 Jefferson, Detroit, MI 48209 (42.299309, -83.096208)
(810) 793-6739, info@historicfortwaynecoalition.com,
www.historicfortwaynecoalition.com
Hours: Mid-Apr to Oct: Sat-Sun 10am-4pm. *Site Info:* On-site parking; $5 per car. Tour guide available; $5/person.

Visitors can tour Fort Wayne's original 1848 limestone barracks building, 1845 star fort that was renovated in 1861, restored commanding officer's house, and Spanish-American War guard house. Also on site is the National Museum of the Tuskegee Airmen, which is open by appointment only; call (313) 833-8849 for more information.

Motown Museum

2648 W. Grand Blvd., Detroit, MI 48208 (42.364239, -83.088494)
(313) 875-2264, info@motownmuseum.org,
www.motownmuseum.org
Hours: Year-round: Tue-Sat 10am-6pm; Jul-Aug: Mon-Fri 10am-6pm, Sat 10am-8pm. *Admission:* Adults $10, Seniors and Children (0-12) $8. *Site Info:* Free street parking. Wheelchair accessible. Tours included in price of admission.

Since 1985, the Motown Museum has been dedicated to preserving the legacy of the Motown Records Corporation through the conservation of Motown's original site in Detroit. Visitors can stand in studio A, where their favorite artists and groups recorded much-loved music, and view the restored upper flat where Berry Gordy lived during the company's earliest days.

Ukrainian American Archives & Museum

11756 Charest St., Detroit, MI 48212 (42.405208, -83.059778)
(313) 366-9764, ukrainianmuseum@sbcglobal.net,
www.ukrainianmuseumdetroit.org
Hours: Tue-Fri 9am-5pm. Also by appointment. *Admission:* $3. *Site Info:* Free street parking. Not wheelchair accessible. Tour guide available. Donations accepted.

The Ukrainian American Archives & Museum educates the general public about the culture, art, and history of Ukrainians, their immigration to the United States, and their contributions to America. Exhibits include paintings, famous personalities, costumes, lectures, artist exhibits, sculptures, and pottery.

Walter P. Reuther Library of Labor and Urban Affairs
Wayne State University, 5401 Cass Ave., Detroit, MI 48202 (42.359011, -83.068866)
(313) 577-4024, reutherreference@wayne.edu,
http://reuther.wayne.edu
Hours: Mon-Fri 10am-4pm. *Admission:* Free. *Site Info:* Metered street parking. Wheelchair accessible. Tour guide available by appointment; contact Reference Archivist William LeFevre.

The Walter P. Reuther Library of Labor and Urban Affairs was established as the Labor History Archives at Wayne State University in 1960, with the goal of collecting and preserving original source materials relating to the development of the American labor movement. Occasionally, the library hosts exhibits in the first floor atrium or along the gallery wall of the Leonard Woodcock Wing. Upcoming and current exhibits are posted on the library's website.

DEXTER

Dexter Area Museum
3443 Inverness St., Dexter, MI 48130 (42.3339049, -83.880052)
(734) 426-2519, dexmuseum@aol.com, www.dextermuseum.org
Hours: May-Nov: Fri-Sat 1-3pm. *Admission:* Free. *Site Info:* Free on-site parking. Not wheelchair accessible. Self-guided.

The Dexter Area Historical Society maintains its museum in the former St. Andrews Church, which was built in 1883. Displays include furniture, clothing, toys, medical equipment, a dentist office, military artifacts from Civil War to WWII, a carriage, farm implements, school materials, and a model railroad layout replicating the Village of Dexter.

Gordon Hall
8347 Island Lake Road, Dexter, MI 48130 (42.342260, -83.897452)
(734) 426-2519, dexmuseum@aol.com, www.dextermuseum.org
Site Info: Free on-site parking. Partially wheelchair accessible, first floor only. Tour guide available during Dexter Days; cost is $5/person. Group tours also available by appointment for a donation.

Built in 1843 for Judge Samuel Dexter, Gordon Hall was once known as one of the most beautiful Greek Revival buildings in Michigan. Today, the Dexter Area Historical Society provides tours discussing the building's history.

DRYDEN

Dryden Historical Depot

5488 Main St., Dryden, MI 48428 (42.945805, -83.125922)
(810) 796-3611, drydenhistoricalsociety@gmail.com,
www.drydenhistoricalsociety.webs.com
Hours: Mon 5:30-7pm. Also by appointment. *Admission:* Donations accepted.

Built in 1883, the Dryden Historical Depot moved to its current location in 1970. It is now used as a museum by the Dryden Historical Society.
*Information may not be current.

DUNDEE

Old Mill Museum

242 Toledo St., Dundee, MI 48131 (41.955418, -83.659021)
(734) 529-8596, www.dundeeoldmill.com
Hours: Fri-Mon 12-4pm. *Admission:* Donations accepted. *Site Info:* Free on-site parking. Wheelchair accessible. Tour guide available; call ahead to schedule a group tour.

A former Henry Ford "Village Industry" factory and gristmill, the Old Mill Museum considers the Ford Village Industries, farm and small-town life in the 19th and 20th centuries, and the Macon Indian Reservation (1808-1828). The museum hosts paranormal tours by reservation on Friday and Saturday nights.

EASTPOINTE

Michigan Military Technical & Historical Society

16600 Stephens Road, Eastpointe, MI 48021 (42.472047, -82.950384)
(586) 872-2581, mimths@mimths.org, www.mimths.org
Hours: Sat 10am-5pm, Sun 12-5pm. *Admission:* $5. *Site Info:* Free on-site parking. Wheelchair accessible. Tour guide available; groups of 10+ are asked to call ahead.

The Michigan Military Technical & Historical Society's museum shares the story of the role played by Michigan's civilian and military personnel in the 20th century and showcases the products of Michigan's "Arsenal of Democracy."

FARMINGTON

Governor Warner Mansion

33805 Grand River Ave., Farmington, MI (42.466662, -83.381502)

(248) 474-5500, *warner_mansion@tds.net,*
www.facebook.com/governor.mansion
Hours: Wed 1-5pm. Also 1st Sun monthly 1-5pm. Call for Dec
hours. *Admission:* Adult $3, Youth (7-12) $1. *Site Info:* Free on-site
and street parking. Not wheelchair accessible. Group tours by
appointment; call (248) 474-5500, ext. 2225.

The Governor Warner Mansion was once home to Frederick
Warner, Michigan's governor from 1905 to 1911. The carriage
house features a classroom, 19th-century tools, and an early 20th-
century printing press and loom.

FARMINGTON HILLS

Holocaust Memorial Center
28123 Orchard Lake Road, Farmington Hills, MI 48334 (42.502101,
-83.359516)
(248) 553-2400, stephen.goldman@holocaustcenter.org,
www.holocaustcenter.org
Hours: Sun-Thu 9:30am-5pm (last admission 3:30pm), Fri 9:30am-
3pm (last admission 12:30pm). Closed Jewish holidays. *Admission:*
Adults $8, Seniors (55+) and University Students $6, Middle and
High School Students $5. Uniformed Service Personnel (i.e., police,
fire, military) are free. See website for group rates. *Site Info:* Free
on-site parking. Wheelchair accessible. Tour guide available Sun-
Thu at 1pm; reservations requested for groups of six or more.

Highlights at the Holocaust Memorial Center include the interactive
Portraits of Honor, where visitors can read and hear the stories of
many of Michigan's survivors; the Institute of the Righteous, which
considers those who risked their lives to help save strangers during
the Holocaust; and a WWII-era boxcar surrounded by an exhibit
reminiscent of the Hamburg-Hannover Bahnhof train station.

FERNDALE

Ferndale Historical Museum
1651 Livernois, Ferndale, MI 48220 (42.459373, -83.143747)
(248) 545-7606, garryandrewsmich@comcast.net,
www.ferndalehistoricalsociety.org
Hours: Mon-Wed 10am-1pm, Sat 1-4pm. Also by appointment.
Admission: Donations accepted. *Site Info:* On-site parking. Partially
wheelchair accessible. Tour guide available; 24 hours notice needed
for special tours.

The Ferndale Historical Museum is housed in a building given to the
city by the Canadian Legion Post No. 71.

FLAT ROCK

Memory Lane Village

25200 Gibraltar Road, Flat Rock, MI 48134 (42.095292, -83.27781)
(734) 782-5220, feskos.fesko13@gmail.com,
www.flatrockhistory.org
Hours: 2nd Sunday monthly 1-4pm. Also by appointment.
Admission: Free. *Site Info:* Free on-site parking shared with Flat
Rock Library. Partially wheelchair accessible. Tour guide available
during open houses and by appointment.

Formed in 1975 to save Munger General store, the Flat Rock
Historical Society now maintains the following historic buildings:
C.J. Munger Store, Flat Rock Hotel, carriage house, DTI caboose,
and the Wagar House. Special exhibits change monthly.

FLINT

Alfred P. Sloan Museum

1221 E. Kearsley St., Flint, MI 48503 (43.023364, -83.6786115
(810) 237-3450, sloan@sloanlongway.org,
www.sloanlongway.org/sloan-museum
Hours: Mon-Fri 10am-5pm, Sat-Sun 12-5pm. *Admission:* Adults $9,
Seniors $8, Youth (3-11) $6, Children (0-2) free. *Site Info:* Free on-
site parking. Wheelchair accessible.

The Sloan Museum features exhibits and displays relating to
regional history, historic automobiles, and hands-on science. In the
"Flint and the American Dream" exhibit, dramatic settings, video
programs, and hundreds of artifacts and photographs portray the
area's tumultuous 20th-century history.

Applewood Estate

1400 E. Kearsley St., Flint, MI 48503 (43.023849, -83.673162)
(810) 233-3835, delliott@ruthmott.org, www.applewood.org
Hours: See website. *Admission:* Free. Please consider bringing food
or personal care items to be donated to local shelters. *Site Info:* On-
site parking; enter on Longway Boulevard. Electric golf carts
provided for those unable to walk long distances. Guided tours
available for groups of 10+; contact Linda Bedtelyon at (810) 233-
3835.

Listed in the National Register of Historic Places, Applewood is the
estate of the Charles Stewart Mott family. Built by Mott in 1916, the
estate features the original home and barn, 34 acres of stately trees,
and the heritage apple orchard for which it was named. Sculptures
on site include Marshall Frederick's "Friendly Frog," Richard Hunt's
"Anvil's Reach," and Chakaiah Booker's "Risky Intentions."

Buick Automotive Gallery and Research Center

303 Walnut St., Flint, MI 48503 (43.025341, -83.675769)
(810) 237-3440, sloan@sloanlongway.org,
www.sloanlongway.org/sloan-museum
Hours: Mon-Fri 10am-5pm, Sat 12-5pm. *Admission:* Adults $9,
Juniors $9. Includes admission to Alfred P. Sloan Museum. *Site
Info:* Free on-site parking. Wheelchair accessible. Self-guided.

The Buick Automotive Gallery and Research Center features more
than 25 classic and concept Buicks, Chevrolets, and other locally
built automobiles. Visitors can relax at the 1940s soda fountain of
Mackenzie's Drug Store, sit behind the wheel of a 1917 Buick
Touring, and observe museum staff and volunteers as they work on
the automotive collection in the new vehicle conservation and
restoration shop.

Crossroads Village & Huckleberry Railroad

5045 Stanley Road, Flint, MI 48506 (43.095060, -83.656167)
(800) 648-7275, parkswebteam@gcparks.org,
www.geneseecountyparks.org
Hours: May-Sep: Wed-Sun and Holidays 10am-5pm. See website
for Oct-Dec hours. *Admission:* Adults $10, Seniors $9, Children $8.
Additional charge for train, boat, and/or amusement rides. Fees vary
for special events. *Site Info:* Free on-site parking. Wheelchair
accessible. Self-guided.

The 51-acre Crossroads Village is home to more than 34 historic
structures, a narrow-gauge steam railroad, and the *Genesee Belle*
paddlewheel riverboat. Visitors can ride the Huckleberry Railroad,
catch a show at the Colwell Opera House, or learn a trade from one
of the many costumed interpreters representing American life in the
1800s.

Durant Dort Carriage Company Headquarters

316 Water St., Flint, MI 48503 (43.016481, -83.697601)
(810) 410-4605, dwhite@kettering.edu, www.geneseehistory.org
Hours: See website or call ahead. *Admission:* Free. *Site Info:* Free
parking behind building. Wheelchair accessible. Tour guide
available by appointment.

The Genesee County Historical Society's museum is located in the
restored Durant Dort Carriage Company Headquarters, the
birthplace of the General Motors Corporation. Today, the building is
a National Historic Landmark that features photo exhibits, carriages,
and furniture.

Whaley Historic House Museum

624 E. Kearsley St., Flint, MI 48503 (43.019886, -83.683933)
(810) 471-4714, 1885@whaleyhouse.com, www.whaleyhouse.com
Hours: Sat 10am-1pm. *Admission:* Adults $5, Children and Students

$3. *Site Info:* Free on-site parking. Partially wheelchair accessible; first floor only. Tour guide available.

The Whaley Historic House Museum was once the home of the prominent Whaley family of Flint. The home now serves as a museum with the mission of spreading the importance of Flint's history to the public, while demonstrating life during Gilded Age America. Listed in the National Register of Historic Places, the building contains many items once owned by the Whaley family and other prominent Flint families.

FLUSHING

Flushing Area Museum and Cultural Center
431 W. Main St., Flushing, MI 48433 (43.062502, -83.861866)
(810) 487-0814, fahs@att.net, www.flushinghistorical.org
Hours: May-Dec 1-4pm. Closed holidays. *Admission:* Free. *Site Info:* Free on-site parking. Wheelchair accessible. Self-guided.

The Flushing Area Historical Society maintains the historical integrity of Flushing's 1888 Grand Trunk depot and operates the facility as a museum and cultural center. The restored structure now features displays on railroading and local history, veterinary medical equipment, drugstore items, 1930s kitchen appliances, and shaving mug display.

FRASER

Baumgartner House and Museum
Hemme Barn
18577 Masonic Ave., Fraser, MI 48026 (42.532252, -82.929783)
(586) 294-6633, www.micityoffraser.com
Hours: Year-round: 1st Sun monthly 1-4pm; Jun and Sep: 2nd Sun monthly. Closed Jan-Feb and Jul. *Admission:* Donations accepted. *Site Info:* On-site parking. Partially wheelchair accessible; depot welcome center and Hemme Barn only. Tour guide available.

Preserved by the Fraser Historical Commission, the Baumgartner House and Museum was built in 1875 in the German architectural style "Rundbogenstil," meaning round, arched style. It features vintage furnishings. Located on the same property is the Hemme Barn, which contains gardening tools and a shoe repair display.

GAGETOWN

Thumb Octagon Barn
6948 Richie Road, Gagetown, MI 48735 (43.670804, -83.217330)
(989) 665-0081, www.thumboctagonbarn.org
Hours: May-Sep: Daily 9am-6pm. Oct: By appointment only.

Admission: Self-guided tours $2, guided tours $5. *Site Info:* Free on-site parking. Wheelchair accessible. Tour guide available upon request.

The 70-foot-high, 8,000-square-foot Octagon Barn was part of "Mud Lake Estate," built by banker James Purdy in the 1920s. The site includes the Craftsman-style Purdy home, a one-room school, grain elevator, blacksmith shop, sawmill, cider mill, wooden walking bridge, powerhouse, etc.

GARDEN CITY

Garden City Historical Museum
6221 Merriman Road, Garden City, MI 48135 (42.330971, -83.351021)
(734) 838-0650, straight.farmhouse@yahoo.com, www.sfhonline.org
Hours: Wed and Sat 12-3pm. *Admission:* Donations accepted. *Site Info:* Free on-site parking. Wheelchair accessible. Tour guide available.

Located in the 1866 Straight Farmhouse, the Garden City Historical Museum contains three floors of exhibits pertaining to the origins of Garden City, a recreation of a 1930s post office, Lathers General Store, and Grande Parlour Banquet Room.

GOODELLS

Historic Village at Goodells County Park
8345 County Park Drive, Goodells, MI 48207 (42.986033, -82.658514)
(810) 325-1146, thewengs@webtv.net; hermweng@gmail.com, www.waleshistoricalsociety.org
Hours: By appointment; call Herman Weng at (810) 325-1146.
Admission: Donations accepted. *Site Info:* Free on-site parking. Wheelchair accessible. Tour guide available.

Attractions at the Historic Village at Goodells County Park include C.C. Peck Bank (c. 1900), Lynn School (c. 1882), Mudge Log Cabin (c. 1860), and Murphy-Ryan Farm (c. 1871). Local family archives—photos, documents, artifacts—are on display in C.C. Peck Bank. The park was once the location of the county's poor farm.

St. Clair County Farm Museum
8310 County Park Drive, Goodells, MI 48027 (42.983033, -82.6551784)
(810) 325-1737, dcporrett@hotmail.com, www.stclaircountyfarmmuseum.org
Hours: Apr-Oct: Hours vary. Also by appointment. *Admission:* Free.

Site Info: Free on-site parking. Not wheelchair accessible. Tour guide available; reservations recommended.

Located in the restored farmhouse in the Historic Village at Goodells County Park, the St. Clair County Farm Museum has a large collection of antique and vintage farming equipment, including horse-drawn and steam-powered examples. The site's primary focus is on the time period between 1880 and 1965, when the county farm was an active agricultural operation.

GRAND BLANC

Grand Blanc Heritage Association Museum
203 E. Grand Blanc Road, Grand Blanc, MI 48439 (42.926422, -83.631250)
(810) 694-7274, dharrett@tir.com, www.cityofgrandblanc.com
Hours: Wed 10am-2pm. *Admission:* Donations accepted. *Site Info:* Free on-site parking. Partially wheelchair accessible. Tour guide available.

Housed in an 1885 Congregational Church, the Grand Blanc Heritage Association Museum is listed in the State Register of Historic Sites. Its exhibit rooms display a restored 1922 player piano, an 1875 reed organ, and other artifacts.

GROSSE ILE

Michigan Central Railroad Depot Museum & Customs House
25020 E. River Road, Grosse Ile, MI 48138 (42.125887, -83.141634)
(734) 675-1250, www.gihistory.org
Hours: Sun 1-4pm, Thu 10am-12pm. *Admission:* Free. *Site Info:* Free on-site parking. Not wheelchair accessible. Self-guided.

Operated by the Grosse Ile Historical Society, the Michigan Central Depot Museum & Customs House contains displays about the railroad, community life, and significant Grosse Ile artifacts.

Grosse Ile Township Hall
9601 Groh Road, Grosse Ile, MI 48138 (42.106699, -83.164497)
(734) 675-1250, www.gihistory.org
Hours: Mon-Fri 8am-5pm. *Admission:* Free. *Site Info:* Free on-site parking. Wheelchair accessible. Self-guided.

Exhibits at the Grosse Ile Township Hall consider naval history and Grosse Ile's legacy as a Naval Air Station through artifacts and photographs.

Grosse Ile North Channel Light

Lighthouse Point Road, Grosse Ile, MI 48138 (42.347015, -82.954308)

(734) 675-1250, www.gihistory.org

Hours: Sep: 2nd Sun. *Admission:* Varies. *Site Info:* Not wheelchair accessible. Tour guide available.

Built in 1894, the North Channel Light is the only remaining light on Grosse Ile.

GROSSE POINTE FARMS

Provencal-Weir House

376 Kercheval Ave., Grosse Pointe Farms, MI 48236 (42.409570, -82.891575)

(313) 884-7010, info@gphistorical.org, www.gphistorical.org

Hours: 2nd Sat monthly 1-4pm. *Admission:* Free. *Site Info:* Not wheelchair accessible. Free street parking. Group tours by appointment.

Built circa 1823, the Provencal-Weir House is believed to be the community's oldest surviving residence. It is now the site of numerous events that recreate life in the early days of Grosse Pointe. Also located on the property is a log cabin dating to the mid-1800s.
Information may not be current.

GROSSE POINTE SHORES

Edsel & Eleanor Ford House

1100 Lake Shore Road, Grosse Pointe Shores, MI 48236 (42.454231, -82.873598)

(313) 884-4222, info@fordhouse.org, www.fordhouse.org

Hours: See website. *Admission:* Adults $12, Seniors $11, Children (6-12) $8, Children (0-5) free. *Site Info:* On-site parking; free except during large grounds events. Partially wheelchair accessible. All tours are guided.

The Edsel & Eleanor Ford House is the former home of automotive pioneer Edsel Ford and his family. Permanent exhibits include the historic garage with Ford family vehicles. Temporary and traveling exhibits explore textiles, nature, art, and other subjects related to the estate and interests of the Fords.
Information may not be current.

HADLEY

Hadley Township Historical Society

3633 Hadley Road, Hadley, MI 48440 (42.954589, -83.403487)

(810) 797-4026, krc@centurytel.net, www.hadleytownship.org

Hours: By appointment. *Admission:* Donations accepted. *Site Info:* On-site parking. Partially wheelchair accessible, lower level only. Tour guide available.

The Hadley Township Historical Society maintains a museum in the former Hadley Flour and Feed Mill. The building features the mill's turbine, grain elevators, lineshaft, and a large engine.

HAMBURG

Hamburg Township Historical Museum

7225 Stone St., Hamburg, MI 48139 (42.449380, -83.802029)
(810) 986-0190, suzanne@pendragon-design.com,
www.hamburg.mi.us
Hours: Wed 4-7pm, Sat 11am-3pm. *Admission:* Donations accepted.
Site Info: Free on-site parking. Wheelchair accessible. Tour guide available.

The Hamburg Township Historical Museum preserves and presents the history of Hamburg through local history displays, active research archives, and changing special exhibits. Permanent galleries depict life in Hamburg since 1831 and include furniture, household items, textiles, farm tools, etc. There is also a military gallery, archive room, and tea room.

HARBOR BEACH

White Rock School Museum

10124 White Rock Road, Harbor Beach, MI 48441 (43.709702, -82.611426)
(989) 864-3817
Hours: By appointment. *Admission:* Free. *Site Info:* Free on-site parking. Wheelchair accessible. Tour guide available by appointment.

Set up as a 1909 schoolhouse with authentic materials, the White Rock School Museum affords educational opportunities and glimpses of the past, when one-room schools were prevalent.

HARTLAND

Florence B. Dearing Museum

3503 Avon St., Hartland, MI 48353 (42.654830, -83.754323)
(810) 229-7621, www.hartlandareahistory.org
Hours: Apr-Oct: Wed 2-4pm, Sat 10am-2pm; Winter: Sat 10am-2pm. *Admission:* $1 donation. *Site Info:* Public parking. Not wheelchair accessible. Tour guide available; donations accepted.

Maintained by the Hartland Area Historical Society, the Florence B. Dearing Museum is located in the former township hall. Its displays relate to farming, blacksmithing, looms (Hartland was noted for its weaving from 1930 to 1970), and the original 1837 Hartland Post Office. The museum also includes an antique kitchen and living room as well as many changing exhibits.

HOLLY

Hadley House Museum

306 S. Saginaw St., Holly, MI 48442 (42.789828, -83.628158)
(248) 634-9233, hollyhistoricalsoc@comcast.net,
www.hollyhistorical.org
Hours: Various Sun 1-4pm. *Admission:* Adults $2. *Site Info:*
Limited parking. Not wheelchair accessible. Self-guided.

Built in 1873, the Hadley House Museum is in the Victorian Italianate style with original woodwork and four bedrooms.The museum, which features its original interior, contains a large local photographic collection, period furniture, and several historical displays.

HOWELL

Howell Area Historical Society Museum

128 Wetmore Street, Howell, MI 48844 (42.609268, -83.929550)
(517) 548-6876, howellareahistoricalsociety@gmail.com,
www.howellareahistoricalsociety.org
Hours: May-Sep: Sun 10am-2pm. Also by appointment. *Admission:*
Donations accepted. *Site Info:* Free on-site parking. Wheelchair accessible. Tour guide available during open hours or by appointment.

Located in the 1886 Ann Arbor depot, the Howell Area Historical Society Museum houses a replica of a general store from the 1890s, artifacts from WWI and WWII, and more. The station master's office has been left almost untouched. The site also features an 1888 Grand Trunk wooden caboose. The depot is listed in the State Register of Historical Sites and the National Register of Historic Places.

HUDSON

Hudson Museum

219 W. Main St., Hudson, MI 49247 (41.854451, -84.354888)
(517) 448-8858
Hours: Mon and Wed 1-4pm, Sat 12-3pm. Also by appointment.
Admission: Donations accepted. *Site Info:* Free on-site parking.
Wheelchair accessible. Tour guide available; large groups can be

accommodated outside of normal business hours and should contact museum well in advance.

The Bean Creek Valley Historical Society operates the Hudson Museum. Attractions include a military exhibit (Civil War to Desert Storm) and a Girl and Boy Scouts exhibit. Items on display relate to medicine, railroad and local industries, theaters, and more.

William G. Thompson House Museum & Gardens
101 Summit St., Hudson, MI 49247 (41.851000, -84.354061)
(517) 448-8125, rlennard@thompsonmuseum.org,
www.thompsonmuseum.org
Hours: Mon, Wed, and Fri 12-3:30pm. Also by appointment.
Admission: Adults $7.50, Seniors and Students $5. *Site Info:* Free on-site parking. Partially wheelchair accessible. Tours are guided.

The William G. Thompson House Museum & Gardens preserves the collections and spirit of William G. Thompson through the interpretation of this three-generational Queen Anne-style home. The 1890 structure is listed in the National Register of Historic Places.

IMLAY CITY

Imlay City Historical Museum
77 Main St., Imlay City, MI 48444 (43.023607, -83.074466)
(810) 724-1904, bswihart1904@charter.net,
www.imlaycityhistoricalmuseum.org
Hours: Apr-Dec: Sat 1-4pm. Also by appointment. *Admission:* Donations accepted. *Site Info:* Street parking. Wheelchair accessible. Self-guided.

Located in the former Grand Trunk Depot, the Imlay City Historical Museum features displays concerning the military, farming, racecar driver Bob Burman, medicine, and more. Exhibits in the main room change periodically. Also on site are a caboose and bunk car.

LAPEER

Davis Brothers Farm Shop Museum
3520 Davis Lake Road, Lapeer, MI 48446 (43.071350, -83.363131)
(810) 245-5808, demlake@charter.net,
www.lapeerhistoricalmuseum.org
Hours: Aug: 4th Sat. Also by appointment. *Admission:* Donations accepted. Call for group pricing. *Site Info:* On-site parking. Wheelchair accessible. Tour guide available; contact Jim Davis at (810) 245-0852 or (810) 441-4803.

The Davis Brothers Farm Shop Museum features several pieces of vintage farm machinery from the early 1900s to the 1950s. Exhibits include hand tools and an operating shop. A restored sawmill operates during the Farm Fest (4th Sat of Aug).

Historic Courthouse
235 W. Nepessing St., Lapeer, MI 48446 (43.054009, -83.310710)
(810) 245-5808, demlake@charter.net,
www.lapeerhistoricalmuseum.org
Hours: May-Oct: Sat 10am-3pm. Also by appointment. *Admission:* Free. Call for group pricing. *Site Info:* Street and public lot parking. Wheelchair accessible. Tour guide available.

Built in 1847, Lapeer's Historic Courthouse is the oldest continuously operating courthouse in Michigan. Exhibits include restoration work and photos/artifacts from the courthouse and early leaders in Lapeer.

Lapeer County Historical Museum
518 W. Nepessing St., Lapeer, MI 48446 (43.053158, -83.314048)
(810) 245-5808, demlake@charter.net,
www.lapeerhistoricalmuseum.org
Hours: Wed and Sat 10am-3pm. Also by appointment for groups. *Admission:* Donations accepted. Call for group pricing.

Permanent exhibits at the Lapeer County Historical Museum include household items and artifacts pertaining to the lumber industry.

LINCOLN PARK

Lincoln Park Historical Society & Museum
1335 Southfield Road, Lincoln Park, MI 48146 (42.250222, -83.178522)
(313) 386-3137, curator@lphistorical.org, www.lphistorical.org
Hours: Wed, Thu, Sat 1-5pm. *Admission:* Free. *Site Info:* Free on-site parking. Wheelchair accessible. Self-guided.

Located in Lincoln Park's former Depression-era post office, the Lincoln Park Historical Society & Museum includes artifacts from local farms, homes, and businesses. Exhibits include a music room and country kitchen. On display are cameras, radios, telephones, and firearms.

LIVONIA

Greenmead Historical Park
20501 Newburgh, Livonia, MI 48152 (42.437496, -83.416442)
(248) 477-7375, greenmead@ci.livonia.mi.us,
www.facebook.com/greenmead

Hours: Tours available Jun-Oct and Dec (no holiday weekends): Sun 1-4pm. Also by appointment. *Site Info:* Free on-site parking. Partially wheelchair accessible. Tours are $3/adult and $2/student.

Greenmead Historical Park is located on the 1820s homestead of Michigan pioneer Joshua Simmons. Today, the park recreates the historic Newburg Intersection, shows what rural life was like in Livonia before urbanization occurred in the 1950s, and includes several historic buildings.

MANCHESTER

John Schneider Blacksmith Shop Museum
324 E. Main St., Manchester, MI 48158 (42.151028, -84.036633)
(517) 536-0775, mahs-info@manchesterareahistoricalsociety.org,
www.manchesterareahistoricalsociety.org
Hours: By appointment. *Admission:* Donations accepted. *Site Info:* Free street parking. Not wheelchair accessible. Tour guide available by appointment.

The Manchester Area Historical Society operates the John Schneider Blacksmith Shop Museum for educational purposes.

MARINE CITY

Community Pride & Heritage Museum
405 South Main St., Marine City, MI 48039 (42.715922, -82.494176)
(810) 765-5446, marinecitymuseum@hotmail.com,
www.marinecitymuseum.org
Hours: Jun-Oct: Sat-Sun 1-4pm. *Admission:* Donations accepted. *Site Info:* Free street parking. Wheelchair accessible. Tour guide available for groups of 10+; appointment via e-mail required.

The Community Pride & Heritage Museum provides information on local history and shipbuilding in the area. The museum is located in the former Newport Academy, which was constructed in 1847 by Eber Brock Ward and run by his sister, Emily. Exhibits touch on shipbuilding, Americana, business, farming, and genealogy research.

MILAN

Friend-Hack House Museum
775 County St., Milan, MI 48160 (42.084674, -83.670411)
(734) 439-1297, farmera44@att.net, www.historicmilan.com
Hours: May-Oct: Sun 1-4pm. *Admission:* Free. *Site Info:* Free on-site parking. Not wheelchair accessible. Tour guide available.

Built in 1888 with ill-gotten funds from a sugar scandal, the Friend-Hack House remained in the Hack family until it was deeded to the city of Milan in the 1970s. Now used as a museum, the building features late 19th-century furnishings and clothing articles. Also on site is a three-hole outhouse, a chicken coop where visitors can view a colony of honeybees at work, and more.

MILLINGTON

Millington-Arbela Historical Society & Museum

8534 State St. (M-15 Heritage Route), Millington, MI 48746 (43.280334, -83.529808)
(989) 871-5508, millingtonarbelahistoricalsociety@hotmail.com, http://millington-arbela-historical-society.webs.com/
Hours: Apr-Dec: Fri-Sat 12-2pm. Also by appointment; call Mel at (810) 871-5508 or Bob at (989) 871-2817. *Admission:* Free. *Site Info:* Free on-site and street parking. Partially wheelchair accessible. Tour guide available; special tours available with 24 hours notice.

The Millington-Arbela Historical Society & Museum preserves the history of the Millington and Arbela area.

MONROE

Eby Log House

3775 S. Custer, Monroe, MI 48161 (41.932166, -83.462083)
(734) 240-7780, history@monroemi.org, www.monroemuseums.org
Hours: Open during Monroe County Fair (end of Jul, beginning of Aug). *Admission:* Free, although admission to the fair is required. *Site Info:* Not wheelchair accessible. Self-guided.

The Eby Log House belonged to the Eby family and dates back to the late 1850s.

Martha Barker Country Store Museum

3815 N. Custer Road, Monroe, MI 48162 (41.935343, -83.461377)
(734) 240-7780, history@monroemi.org, www.monroemuseums.org
Hours: Seasonal. *Admission:* Donations accepted. *Site Info:* Free on-site parking. Wheelchair accessible. Self-guided.

Located in the former one-room Papermill School (1860s-1962), the Martha Barker Country Store Museum features a collection of local mercantile objects (c. 1910). The site is part of a complex with the Navarre-Anderson Trading Post and supplies the parking lot for both sites.

Monroe County Historical Museum

126 S. Monroe St., Monroe, MI 48161 (41.915064, -83.398938)
(734) 240-7780, history@monroemi.org, www.monroemuseums.org

Hours: Year-round: Wed-Sat 10am-5pm; Summer: Wed-Sat 10am-5pm, Sun 12-5pm. Also by appointment. *Admission:* Suggested donations: Adults (18+), youth (6-17) $2, Children (0-5) free. *Site Info:* Limited free on-site parking; metered street parking. Wheelchair accessible. Self-guided.

The Monroe County Historical Museum focuses on the county's Native Americans, early French inhabitants, and military history. Exhibits also consider life on Lake Erie and the River Raisin, George and Libbie Custer, and several other aspects of Monroe County's history.

Monroe County Vietnam Veterans Museum

Heck Park, North Dixie Hwy and Circle Drive, Monroe, MI 48161 (41.925430, -83.367165)
(734) 240-7780, history@monroemi.org, www.monroemuseums.org
Hours: May-Sep: Wed and Sat 12-4pm. *Admission:* Donations accepted. *Site Info:* On-site parking. Wheelchair accessible. Group tours available by appointment; call (734) 240-7780.

Staffed by Monroe County Vietnam War veterans, this museum displays more than 1,500 artifacts: news releases, stories of local soldiers, sailors and airmen, magazine articles, medals/ribbons, models, dioramas, Vietnamese artifacts, and military uniforms from the Vietnam War.

Navarre-Anderson Trading Post Complex

3775 N. Custer, Monroe, MI 48162 (41.935021, -83.460295)
(734) 240-7780, history@monroemi.org, www.monroemuseums.org
Hours: Seasonal and by appointment. *Admission:* Donations accepted. *Site Info:* Free on-site parking. Partially wheelchair accessible. Self-guided.

The Navarre-Anderson Trading Post (c. 1790s) was moved to its current site on the River Raisin as part of a French "ribbon" farm and is one of two original buildings. It has been interpreted as a French fur trade business and home, as it had been used. The Navarre-Morris cabin (c. 1810) is interpreted next to the trading post as a French summer kitchen. There are other farm-related objects on site, including a reproduction barn, beehive oven, and small orchard.

River Raisin National Battlefield Park

1403 E. Elm Ave., Monroe, MI 48162 (41.911223, -83.376805)
(734) 243-7136, www.nps.gov/RIRA
Hours: Visitors Center: 10am-5pm; Grounds: Sunrise to sunset. *Admission:* Free. *Site Info:* On-site parking. Wheelchair accessible. Tour guide available by appointment.

The River Raisin National Battlefield Park remembers the battles and sacrifices made along the banks of the River Raisin by preserving and interpreting the significance of the battles of January 1813. The park's visitors center includes exhibits and map orientation. A battlefield walking trail features interpretive signs and a heritage trail that connects to Sterling State Park.

MONTROSE

Montrose Historical & Telephone Pioneer Museum
144 East Hickory St., Montrose, MI 48457 (43.176976, -83.890707)
(810) 639-6644, staff@montrosemuseum.com,
www.montrosemuseum.com
Hours: Sun 1-5pm, Mon-Tue 9am-3pm. *Admission:* Free. *Site Info:* Parking in lot. Wheelchair accessible. Tour guide available. Group tours are $2/adult; children are free.

Originally the telephone office for Public Service Telephone Co., the Montrose Historical & Telephone Pioneer Museum contains hands-on, working exhibits of antique telephone equipment and historical highlights of Montrose. More than 400 telephones are on display.
Information may not be current.

MOUNT CLEMENS

Crocker House Museum
15 Union St., Mount Clemens, MI 48043 (42.598662, -82.881912)
(586) 465-2488, crockerhousemuseum@sbcglobal.net,
www.crockerhousemuseum.com
Hours: Mar-Dec: Tue-Thu 10am-4pm, 1st Sun monthly 1-4pm. Closed holidays. *Admission:* Suggested donation: Adults $3, Children $1. *Site Info:* Metered city parking lot and free street parking. Not wheelchair accessible. Tours are guided.

Operated by the Macomb County Historical Society, the 1869 Crocker House Museum offers a late Victorian home-life experience reminiscent of Mount Clemens' Mineral Bath Era. This home housed the first two mayors of Mount Clemens and later offered a small gambling and lunch room.

Michigan Transit Museum
200 Grand Ave., Mount Clemens, MI 48043 (42.598855, -82.892002)
(586) 463-1863, mtm1973@juno.com,
www.michigantransitmuseum.org
Hours: Sat-Sun 1-4pm. *Admission:* Donations accepted. *Site Info:* Free on-site parking. Wheelchair accessible. Tour guide available; reservations can be made for after-hour tours.

One of the original Grand Trunk Railway stations, the Mount Clemens Depot originally opened for business November 21, 1859. Today, it is home to the Michigan Transit Museum, which is dedicated to the preservation of the history and legacy of railways, streetcars, and the electric interurban in Southeastern Michigan. The museum also offers train excursions that depart from Joy Park on Joy Boulevard. See website for train schedule and ticket fare.

NEW BOSTON

Samuel Adams Historical Museum

37236 Huron River Drive, New Boston, MI 48164 (42.162639, -83.401189)
(734) 753-3109, nfaydee@yahoo.com
Hours: First Sun monthly 1-3pm. *Admission:* Free. *Site Info:* Free on-site parking. Wheelchair accessible. Tour guide available.

Operated by the Huron Township Historical Society, the Samuel Adams Historical Museum is furnished in the style of 1855.

NORTHVILLE

Mill Race Historical Village

215 Griswold Ave., Northville, MI 48167 (42.432708, -83.478889)
(248) 348-1845, mrv1845@yahoo.com, www.millracenorthville.org
Hours: Mid-Jun to mid-Oct: Sun 1-4pm. *Admission:* Free. *Site Info:* Free on-site parking. Partially wheelchair accessible. Self-guided.

The Northville Historical Society created Mill Race Village to preserve examples of architectural styles common to Northville pre-1900. The village is home to 10 relocated, reproduced, and/or reconstructed buildings. Among them are a blacksmith shop, interurban station, Georgian home furnished in the style of 1860, and a home (c. 1890) used as a weaving studio.

OAKLAND

Caretaker House at Cranberry Lake Farm Historic District

384 W. Predmore Road, Oakland, MI 48363 (42.784656, -83.147237)
(248) 652-0712, thsbarkham@hotmail.com,
www.oaklandtownshiphistoricalsociety.org
Hours: Call for hours. *Admission:* Free. *Site Info:* Free on-site parking. Wheelchair accessible. Tour guide available by appointment; donations accepted.

The Oakland Township Historical Society supports Cranberry Lake Farm Historic District, which has nine structures. The society's museum is housed in the caretaker house, which has period furniture representing Victorian through Arts and Craft styles. Farm implements are on display in the rebuilt Flumerfelt barn. The society also periodically develops traveling history exhibits that are displayed at locations including the Paint Creek Cider Mill, Rochester Hills Library, and Older Persons' Commission.

ORCHARD LAKE

Orchard Lake Museum

3951 Orchard Lake Road, Orchard Lake, MI 48323 (42.582809, -83.359433)
(248) 757-2451, gina@gwbhs.org, www.gwbhs.org
Hours: 2nd Sun monthly 1-4pm. Also by appointment. *Admission:* Free. *Site Info:* Free on-site parking. Wheelchair accessible. Tour guide available on open house days; call ahead to schedule a special tour.
The Orchard Lake Museum has a number of artifacts illustrating the history of West Bloomfield Township and the cities of Keego Harbor, Orchard Lake Village, and Sylvan Lake.

Polonica Americana Research Institute (PARI)

3535 Indian Trail, Orchard Lake, MI 48306 (42.595041, -83.356195)
(248) 683-0323, cjensen@mipolonia.net, www.polishmission.com
Hours: Mon-Tue and Fri 10am-4pm. Call for additional hours. *Admission:* Varies. *Site Info:* Free on-site parking. Wheelchair accessible. Tour guide available; tours range in price from $10 to $25 per person.

Part of Orchard Lake Schools, the Polish Mission preserves and promotes Polish and Polish-American culture, tradition, and history for present and future generations. The Museums, Archives, and Library are cornerstones of the Polish Mission's rich history. One highlight is the Polish Panorama, which features 106 handmade figurines that dramatize the history of Poland from its beginning through such major events as the election of Pope John Paul II and the rise of the Solidarity movement.

ORTONVILLE

The Old Mill

366 Mill St., Ortonville, MI 48462 (42.852300, -83.444616)
(248) 627-3893, jmiracle60@comcast.net, www.ortonvillecommunityhistoricalsoc.weebly.com
Hours: Sat 10am-2pm. Also by appointment. *Admission:* Free. *Site Info:* Free on-site and street parking. Not wheelchair accessible. Tour guide available.

The Ortonville Community Historical Society's museum is located in a former gristmill built in 1856 by the town's founder, Amos Orton. The museum includes a working rug loom, Lakota Indian clothing and photos, military memorabilia, and more. Also on site is the Mann One-Room School, which was used until the 1940s and relocated to its present location in 1985.

OXFORD

Northeast Oakland Historical Museum
1 N. Washington St., Oxford, MI 48371 (42.824849, -83.265317)
(248) 628-8413, info@neohs.net, www.neohs.net
Hours: Sat 1-4pm; Jun-Aug: Wed 1-4pm. Also by appointment.
Admission: Donations accepted. *Site Info:* Free parking. Self-guided. Group tours by appointment.

Located in the former Oxford Savings Bank, the Northeast Oakland Historical Museum is home to thousands of items ranging from quilts to farm tools.
Information may not be current.

PIGEON

Pigeon Depot Museum
59 S. Main St., Pigeon, MI 48755 (43.828977, -83.269704)
(989) 453-2214, eschdenny@yahoo.com,
www.thehchs.org/pigeonhs/index.htm
Hours: May-Sep: Mon-Fri 10am-3pm, Sat 10am-12pm. Call for special hours. *Admission:* Donations accepted. *Site Info:* Free public parking lot. Wheelchair accessible.

The Pigeon Depot Museum is located in a former railroad depot. Items on display include a reed organ, pianola, hand tools, household items, turn-of-the-century clothing, railroad artifacts, 4,000 obituary cards, photos, and plat books.

PLYMOUTH

Jarvis-Stone School and Dickerson Barn
7991 N. Territorial Road, Plymouth, MI 48170 (42.367432, -83.607748)
(248) 486-0669, salem_area_hs@yahoo.com, www.sahshistory.org
Hours: May-Sep: 2nd Sun monthly 1-3pm. *Admission:* Free. *Site Info:* Free on-site parking. Wheelchair accessible. Self-guided.

The Salem Area Historical Society owns the property at the northwest corner of North Territorial and Curtis Road, which includes the 1857 Jarvis Stone School, a one-room stone school, and the 1830 Dickerson Barn.

Plymouth Historical Museum

155 S. Main St., Plymouth, MI 48170 (42.372707, -83.466951)
(734) 455-8940, director@plymouthhistory.org,
www.plymouthhistory.org
Hours: Wed and Fri-Sun 1-4pm. *Admission:* Adult $5, Students (6-17) $2. *Site Info:* Free street parking. Wheelchair accessible. Self-guided. Tour guide available by appointment.

The Plymouth Historical Museum features a late 19th-century Victorian recreation of Main Street, tracing the growth of a small town from the railroad depot to the general store; a series of displays of America's history as witnessed by the Plymouth community, from days when native tribes settled in the area to modern times; and the Dr. Weldon Petz Abraham Lincoln Collection.

PONTIAC

Pine Grove Historical Museum

405 Cesar E. Chavez Ave., Pontiac, MI 48342 (42.648109,

-83.304845)
(248) 338-6732, office@ocphs.org, www.ocphs.org
Hours: By appointment. *Admission:* $5. *Site Info:* Free on-site parking. Partially wheelchair accessible; Wisner House is not. Tour guide available by appointment.

The Oakland County Pioneer and Historical Society maintains Pine Grove, which includes the 1845 Greek Revival home of former Michigan Governor Moses Wisner. It also is home to several outbuildings (a root cellar, summer kitchen, smokehouse, and privy), the grove and gardens, the 1865 Drayton Plains One Room School, and the Pioneer Museum, featuring artifacts from the area's rural past.

PORT AUSTIN

Port Austin History Center

1424 Pte. Aux Barques Road, Port Austin, MI 48467 (44.049751, -82.970911)
(989) 551-5532, portaustinareahistoricalsociety@yahoo.com,
www.portaustinhistorycenter.com
Hours: Apr-May: Sat-Sun 1-4pm; Jun-Aug: Daily 10am-4pm; Sep-Dec: Sat-Sun 1-4pm. *Admission:* Free. *Site Info:* Free on-site parking. Wheelchair accessible. Tour guide available; large groups should call in advance.

Exhibits at the Port Austin History Center highlight the Great Fire of 1881, Grindstone City, Port Crescent, Port Austin Reef Lighthouse, and the Great Lakes Storm of 1913/*Howard M. Hanna Jr.* History displays also relate to Port Austin's merchants/businesses, manufacturing, senior school photos and sports trophies, Air Force Station, and more.

PORT HURON

Port Huron Museum
1115 Sixth St., Port Huron, MI 48060 (42.972254, -82.426514)
(810) 982-0891, info@phmuseum.org, www.phmuseum.org
Hours: Wed-Sat 11am-4pm. *Admission:* Adults $7, Seniors and Students $5, Children (0-4) free. Group rates available for 20+; call (810) 982-0891, ext. 118. *Site Info:* Free on-site and street parking. Wheelchair accessible. Self-guided.

Built in 1904 by Andrew Carnegie, the former Port Huron Public Library is now home to the Port Huron Museum. With an emphasis on the maritime and local heritage of the Blue Water Area, the Port Huron Museum shares exhibits about Great Lakes shipping and includes Russell Sawyer's photographs of local history.

Fort Gratiot Light Station
2802 Omar St., Port Huron, MI 48060 (43.005698, -82.424433)
(810) 982-0891, info@phmuseum.org, www.phmuseum.org
Hours: See website for hours. *Admission:* Tours are $7/person. Group rates available for 20+; call (810) 982-0891, ext. 118 for reservations. *Site Info:* Partially wheelchair accessible.

Built in 1829, the Fort Gratiot Light Station is the oldest lighthouse in Michigan and reopened to the public in 2012. For information about the overnight program, e-mail *avarty@phmuseum.org*.

Huron Lightship
North side of Pine Grove Park (at the end of Prospect Place), Port Huron, MI 48060 (42.989549, -82.426616)
(810) 982-0891, info@phmuseum.org, www.phmuseum.org
Hours: See website for hours. *Admission:* Adults $7, Seniors and Students $5, Children (0-4) free. Group rates available for 20+; call (810) 982-0891, ext. 118 for reservations. *Site Info:* Free street parking. Not wheelchair accessible.

The Huron Lightship was a "floating lighthouse" and spent its entire career on the Great Lakes with 36 years in Port Huron. Retired in 1970, the ship has been refinished as a museum and traces the history of its service and those who served. There is a Fog Horn Sounding on Memorial Day, Independence Day, and Labor Day.

Knowlton's Ice Museum of North America
317 Grand River Ave., Port Huron, MI 48060 (42.977519, -82.423020)

*(810) 987-5441, knowltonsicemuseum@yahoo.com,
www.knowltonsicemuseum.org*
Hours: Jun-Sep: Thu-Sat 11am-5pm. *Admission:* Adults $5, Seniors
$4, Children (6-10) $2, Children (0-5) free. *Site Info:* Free on-site
and street parking. Wheelchair accessible. Tour guide available for
groups of 10+.

The 10,000-square-foot Knowlton's Ice Museum of North America
shares the history of the ice harvesting industry. It has one of the
largest collections in the U.S. of ice tools and implements from the
mid-1800s to the early 1900s—a time when most American
households had an ice box and the ice delivery man brought ice by
horse and wagon. Visitors can view rare video footage of a 1920s
ice harvest and have a try at the hands-on activities.

Thomas Edison Depot Museum
510 Edison Parkway, Port Huron, MI 48060 (42.989786,
-82.427287)
(810) 982-0891, info@phmuseum.org, www.phmuseum.org
Hours: See website. *Admission:* Adults $7, Seniors and Students $5,
Children (0-4) free. Group rates available for 20+; call (810) 982-
0891, ext. 118 for reservations. *Site Info:* Free on-site parking.
Wheelchair accessible. Self-guided.

The Fort Gratiot Station of the Grand Trunk Railroad, now known
as the Thomas Edison Depot, is where a teenage Thomas Edison
worked during his years in Port Huron and conducted some of his
early experiments. A restored baggage car recreates his mobile
chemistry lab. There are also interactive displays, experiments, and
films about Edison.

PORT SANILAC

Sanilac County Historic Village and Museum
228 S. Ridge St. (M-25), Port Sanilac, MI 48469 (43.437979,
-82.544123)
*(810) 622-9946, sanilacmuseum@gmail.com,
www.sanilaccountymuseum.org*
Hours: Jun-Aug: Wed-Sun 10:30am-4:30pm. *Admission:* Varies by
event. *Site Info:* Free on-site parking. Wheelchair accessible. Tour
guide available.

Located on the 1853 estate of Dr. Joseph Loop, the Sanilac County
Historic Village and Museum includes 16 historic buildings,
including Loop's Victorian mansion, a hunting and fishing cabin,
and a dairy museum.

RICHMOND

Richmond Historic Village

36045 Park St., Richmond, MI 48062 (42.813294, -82.755220)
(586) 727-7773, richmondareahistoricalsociety@gmail.com,
www.richmondhistoricalsociety.org
Hours: Thu mornings. Also by appointment. *Admission:* Donations
accepted. *Site Info:* Free on-site and street parking. Wheelchair
accessible. Tour guide available; donations accepted.

Operated by the Richmond Area Historical and Genealogical
Society, the Richmond Historic Village consists of a one-room
schoolhouse, train depot, log cabin, and museum with displays that
change bi-annually.

ROCHESTER

Meadow Brook Hall

480 S. Adams Road, Rochester, MI 48309 (42.675557, -83.193926)
(248) 364-6200 , www.meadowbrookhall.org
Hours: Daily 11am-4pm. *Admission:* Adults $15, Seniors (62+) $10,
Oakland University Faculty/Staff/ Alumni with ID $10, OU/Cooley
Students with ID free, Children (0-12) free. *Site Info:* On-site
parking. Wheelchair accessible. Tours are guided; see website for
tour schedule.

Meadow Brook Hall is the former residence of Matilda Dodge
Wilson and her second husband, Alfred Wilson. Constructed
between 1926 and 1929, the 80,000-square-foot mansion represents
one of the finest examples of Tudor-revival architecture in America.
Information may not be current.

World War II Honor Roll Monument

400 Sixth St., Rochester, MI 48307 (42.683337, -83.137215)
(248) 266-5400, rahsupdates@gmail.com,
www.rochesteravonhistoricalsociety.org
Hours: 24 hours/7 days a week. *Admission:* Free. *Site Info:* Free
street parking. Wheelchair accessible. Self-guided.

Originally dedicated by the Blue Star Mothers in 1945, the World
War II Honor Roll Monument was dismantled in 1963. The 16
engraved Carrera glass panels were later found, repaired, some
replicated, restored, and rededicated in 2002. More than 1,100
names of local residents from the Rochester area who fought in
World War II are listed. Located on the east side of City Hall and
lighted, the site is accessible at all times.

ROCHESTER HILLS

Rochester Hills Museum at Van Hoosen Farm

1005 Van Hoosen Road, Rochester Hills, MI 48306 (42.696597, -83.115927)

(248) 656-4663, rhmuseum@rochesterhills.org; dunhamm@rochesterhills.org, www.rochesterhills.org/museum
Hours: Fri-Sat 1-4pm. Also by appointment. *Admission:* Adults $5, Seniors and Students $3. *Site Info:* Free on-site parking. Wheelchair accessible. Tour guide available.

The Rochester Hills Museum at Van Hoosen Farm is a local history museum that focuses on the lives of the Taylor-Van Hoosen families who settled a portion of the community in 1823. Located within Stony Creek Village (a collection of privately owned, pre-Civil War homes listed in the National Register of Historic Places), the site was home to five generations of the Van Hoosen family.

ROCKWOOD

Rockwood Area Historical Society

32787 Wood St., Rockwood, MI 48173 (42.070080, -83.250325)
(734)379-0674, jequick@sbcglobal.net, Find on Facebook
Hours: Sun and Tue 1-3pm. *Admission:* Donations accepted. *Site Info:* Wheelchair accessible.

The Rockwood Area Historical Society's museum building is a replica of the 1869 Rockwood railroad depot. Exhibits change about three times a year. Other attractions include the restoration of a 1968 ICG caboose, which is available for tours at no cost.

ROMEO

Bancroft-Stranahan Home

132 Church St., Romeo, MI 48065 (42.804343, -83.014755)
(586) 752-4111, www.romeohistoricalsociety.org
Hours: Tue 7-9pm. Also by appointment. *Site Info:* Wheelchair accessible.

This 1868 Greek revival was used by the Bancroft and Stranahan families of Romeo. It has period settings that include furniture, clothing, kitchenware, and changing displays. It also has a collection of oil paintings by William Gibbs.
Information may not be current.

Clyde Craig Blacksmith Museum

301 N. Bailey St., Romeo, MI 48065 (42.805638, -83.012205)
(586) 752-4111, www.romeohistoricalsociety.org
Hours: By appointment. *Site Info:* Wheelchair accessible.

Originally built in the 19th century, the Clyde Craig Blacksmith Museum is now a working blacksmith shop/museum. Using the 2,800-degree forge, smiths still utilize the old tools to shape metal. *Information may not be current.*

Romeo Arts & Archives Center

290 N. Main Street, Romeo, MI 48065 (42.805144, -83.013116)
(586) 752-4111, www.romeohistoricalsociety.org
Hours: Tue 7-9pm. Also by appointment. *Admission:* Free. *Site Info:* Wheelchair accessible. On-site and street parking. Staff available for tours.

The Romeo Arts & Archives Center is located in the former Romeo Michigan State Police Post, which was in use from 1936 to 2000. Changing displays interpret Romeo's past.
Information may not be current.

ROYAL OAK

Royal Oak Historical Society Museum

1411 W. Webster Road, Royal Oak, MI 48073 (42.511239, -83.161315)
(248) 439-1501, curator@royaloakhistoricalsociety.org, www.royaloakhistoricalsociety.org
Hours: Tue, Thu, and Sat 1-4pm. Also by appointment. *Admission:* $2 donation. *Site Info:* Free on-site parking. Wheelchair accessible. Tour guide available by appointment; $2 donation/person.

Located in the former Northwood Fire Station, the Royal Oak Historical Society Museum displays rotating exhibits covering the history of Royal Oak from its beginnings as a township in the early 1820s to today as a city.

ST. CLAIR SHORES

Selinksy-Green Farmhouse Museum

22500 Eleven Mile Road, St. Clair Shores, MI 48081 (42.496485, -82.888541)
(586) 771-9020 x271, stachowm@libcoop.net, www.scslibrary.org/sgfm.html
Hours: Sep-May: Wed and Sat 1-4pm; Jun-Aug: Wed 1-4pm.
Admission: Donations are accepted. *Site Info:* Free street and on-site parking. Not wheelchair accessible. Tour guide available during regular hours and by appointment.

Located behind the St. Clair Shores Public Library, the Selinsky-Green Farmhouse is furnished to the period between the 1880s to 1910. The original owners were German and Polish immigrants to the St. Clair Shores area. The house is a saltbox-style split log house covered with clapboard siding. The woodburning stove is operational and used for special baking days.

SALINE

Saline District Library's Meredith Bixby Exhibits

555 N. Maple Road, Saline, MI 48176 (42.177183, -83.775698)
(734) 429-5450, leslee@salinelibrary.org, www.salinelibrary.org
Hours: Mon-Thu 9am-9pm, Fri-Sat 10am-5pm, Sun 1pm-5pm.
Admission: Free. *Site Info:* Free on-site parking. Wheelchair accessible. Self-guided.

Two exhibits at the Saline District Library celebrate Meredith Bixby, a local puppeteer who donated his collection to the city of Saline. Bixby was one of America's foremost puppeteers who traveled from 1930 to 1980. One exhibit shows the construction of a marionette and the other depicts a scene from one of his plays. The scene exhibit changes throughout the year.

Rentschler Farm Museum

1265 E. Michigan Ave., Saline, MI 48176 (42.175966, -83.761197)
(734) 944-0442, salinehistory@frontier.com, www.salinehistory.org
Hours: May to mid-Dec: Sat 11am-3pm. *Admission:* Free. *Site Info:* Free on-site parking. Partially wheelchair accessible; first floor only. Tour guide available; groups of 10+ require a reservation and cost $1/person.

The Rentschler Farm Museum features 12 farm buildings with furnishings respective to the early 20th century. Built in 1906, the 12-room, Queen Anne-style farmhouse has never been changed, with the exception of paint color. It shows life as it was during the Great Depression.

Saline Railroad Depot Museum

402 N. Ann Arbor St., Saline, MI 48176 (42.171506, -83.784297)
(734) 944-0442, salinehistory@frontier.com, www.salinehistory.org
Hours: Sat 11am-3pm. *Admission:* Free. *Site Info:* Free on-site parking. Partially wheelchair accessible. Tour guide available; groups of 10 or more require a reservation and cost $1/person.

The Saline Railroad Depot was built in 1872 and used by the railroad until the 1960s. Exhibits focus on Saline history, especially during the 19th century. There is a furnished station agent's office, caboose, and livery barn.

SEBEWAING

Charles W. Liken House

325 N. Center St., Sebewaing, MI 48759 (43.734856, -83.450136)

(989) 883-2391, beegee38@sbcglobal.net,
www.thehchs.org/sebewaing
Hours: May-Nov: 1st Sat and 1st Sun monthly. *Admission:* Free.
Site Info: Free on-site and street parking. Not wheelchair accessible.
Tour guide available; reservations can be made for after hours.

Maintained by the Sebewaing Area Historical Society, the Charles
W. Liken House was built in the early 1880s by the town's founding
father. The home has since been renovated and now features
replicated versions of the original furnishings.

Old Sebewaing Township Hall
92 S. Center St., Sebewaing, MI 48759 (43.731631, -83.451920)
(989) 883-2391, beegee38@sbcglobal.net,
www.thehchs.org/sebewaing
Hours: May-Nov: 1st Sat and 1st Sun monthly. *Admission:* Free.
Site Info: Free on-site and street parking. Not wheelchair accessible.
Tour guide available; reservations can be made for after hours.

The Old Sebewaing Township Hall has displays pertaining to the
old jail, area businesses, hunting, and doctors. Located next to this
museum is the Rev. J.L. Hahn House, which is in the process of
being repaired and renovated.

SHELBY TOWNSHIP

Packard Proving Grounds Historic Site
49965 Van Dyke Ave., Shelby Township, MI 48317 (42.661685,
-83.036193)
(586) 739-4800, www.packardmotorfdn.org
Site Info: Free on-site parking. Wheelchair accessible. Group tours
available by appointment; costs vary.

The Packard Motor Car Foundation shares the history of the Packard
Motor Car Company. The Packard Proving Grounds Historic Site
features seven buildings built between 1929 and 1942. Six of these
buildings were designed by Albert Kahn. On display are a collection
of Packard automobiles and marine engines, the Miss America X
mahogany racing boat, and more.

SOUTH LYON

Green Oak Township Historical Society
10789 Silver Lake Road, South Lyon, MI 48178 (42.468748,
-83.731793)
(248) 486-9121, jowilliams@aol.com; gail.huck@charter.net,
www.greenoaktownshiphistoricalsociety.org
Hours: By appointment. *Admission:* Donations accepted. *Site Info:*

On-site parking. Wheelchair accessible. Tour guide available upon request.

The Green Oak Township Historical Society Museum is located adjacent to the original Green Oak Township Hall, which was built in 1856. The museum features artifacts from the 1800s.

SOUTHFIELD

Mary Thompson Farm House
25630 Evergreen Road, Southfield, MI 48075 (42.477554, -83.238176)
(248) 356-7788, historicsouthfield@gmail.com,
http://southfieldhistoricalsociety.wordpress.com
Hours: By appointment or during special events. *Admission:* Donations accepted. *Site Info:* Free on-site parking. Partially wheelchair accessible; first floor only. Tour guide available during special events or by appointment; donations accepted.

Exhibits at the Mary Thompson Farm House include furniture and belongings of both Southfield teacher and benefactor Mary Thompson and Jean McDonnell, the first councilwoman for the City of Southfield.

Town Hall Museum
26080 Berg Road, Southfield, MI 48033 (42.480841, -83.279419)
(248) 356-7788, historicsouthfield@gmail.com,
http://southfieldhistoricalsociety.wordpress.com
Hours: During summer concerts Jul-Aug; check *www.cityofsouthfield.com* for dates. Also by appointment. *Admission:* Donations accepted. *Site Info:* Free on-site parking. Wheelchair accessible. Tour guide available during summer concerts or by appointment; donations accepted.

Operated by the Southfield Historical Society, the Town Hall Museum is located at the original site of the 1872 Town Hall. Exhibits consider World War I, the Martin Luther King Task Force, schools in Southfield, and early aviator and test pilot Harry Brooks. Brooks worked for Henry Ford and flew both the Ford Flivver and the Ford Tri-Motor.

ST. CLAIR

St. Clair Historical Museum
308 S. Fourth St., St.Clair, MI 48079 (42.823007, -82.488864)
(810) 329-6888, robert.freehan@gmail.com,
www.historicstclair.com
Hours: Year-round: Tue 9:30am-12pm; May-Nov: Sat-Sun 1:30-4:30pm. *Admission:* Donations accepted. *Site Info:* Free on-site

parking. Not wheelchair accessible. Tour guide available; prior arrangement needed for groups.

The St. Clair Historical Museum has a shoe shop display, Diamond Crystal Salt Company room, and maritime exhibit.

STERLING HEIGHTS

William Upton House
40433 Utica Road, Sterling Heights, MI 48313 (42.591787, -83.011075)
(586) 446-2640, turgeont@libcoop.net,
www.shpl.net/commission.htm
Hours: Open during Sterlingfest (Jul) and Sterling Christmas (Dec). Also by appointment. *Admission:* Free. *Site Info:* Parking in city lot. Partially wheelchair accessible; first floor only.

The Sterling Heights Historical Commission arranges displays in the 1867 Upton House.

TAYLOR

Taylor Historical Museum
12405 Pardee Rd Taylor, MI 48180 (42.216026, -83.252667)
87-3835
Admission: Free. *Site Info:* On-site parking. Wheelchair accessible. Tour guide available.

The Taylor Historical Museum is located in the 1926 Knope Farmhouse in Taylor Heritage Park. Exhibits and history artifacts showcase early Taylor businesses and family life in rural Taylor Township. Also on site is a one-room schoolhouse, historical church, 1850s log cabin, and more.

TECUMSEH

Tecumseh Area Historical Museum
302 E. Chicago Blvd., Tecumseh, MI 49286 (42.004061, -83.941872)
(517) 423-2374, historictecumseh@gmail.com, Find on Facebook
Hours: Apr-Oct: Sat 10:30am-3:30pm. *Admission:* Free. *Site Info:* Free on-site parking. Wheelchair accessible. Self-guided.

Located in the Gothic-style St. Elizabeth Catholic Church, the Tecumseh Area Historical Museum houses materials that illustrate the area's history.

TEMPERANCE

Banner Oak School

Sterns and Crabb Roads, Temperance, MI 48182 (41.750407, -83.547973)

(734) 847-7780, lindaski@buckeye-access.com

Hours: Apr-Oct: By appointment. *Admission:* Free. *Site Info:* Free on-site parking. Wheelchair accessible. Tour guide available by appointment.

The Bedford Historical Society collects and preserves the history of Bedford Township. Attractions include the restored 1871 Banner Oak One-room School.

TRENTON

Trenton Historical Museum

306 St. Joseph, Trenton, MI 48183 (42.140563, -83.179861)

(734) 675-2130, www.trentonhistoricalcommission.org

Hours: Mar-Dec: Sat 1pm-4pm. *Admission:* Donations accepted. *Site Info:* Parking on 3rd Street and St. Joseph. Not wheelchair accessible. Self-guided.

The Trenton Historical Museum is located in a Victorian-style home, which was built in 1881 by John and Sarah Moore. Decorated in the Victorian period, the museum contains information and artifacts relating to Trenton's history.

TROY

Troy Historic Village & Museum

60 W. Wattles Road, Troy, MI 48098 (42.577964, -83.14948)

(248) 524-3570, info@troyhistory.org, www.troyhistoricvillage.org

Hours: Year-round: Mon-Fri 10am-3pm; Summer: Sat. *Admission:* Adults $5, Seniors and Children (5-12) $3. *Site Info:* Free on-site and street parking. Wheelchair accessible. Self-guided.

The Troy Historic Village is a four-acre cultural and educational destination that includes 10 historic buildings, surrounding a traditional village green that is enhanced by gardens and mature trees.

UBLY

The Ten Cent Barn

1 Longuski Drive, Ubly, MI 48475 (43.702505, -82.939513)

(989) 553-4892, ublyareahistoricalsociety@gmail.com, www.thehchs.org

Hours: Memorial Day to Labor Day: Sun 1-4pm. *Admission:* Donations accepted. *Site Info:* Free on-site parking. Partially wheelchair accessible; first floor only. Tour guide available; for a weekday tour, call Leila Korotounova at (989) 553-4892.

Operated by the Ubly Area Historical Society, the Ten Cent Barn includes a blacksmith shop display, farm tools, household items, and historical furniture. During Homecoming Weekend in July, the museum has a "people mover" pulled by an antique tractor taking visitors to and from Memorial Park.

VASSAR

Vassar Museum
Vassar Museum, 450 S. Main St., Vassar, MI 48768 (43.366713, -83.588329)
(989) 823-2651, www.vassarhistory.org
Hours: Apr-Dec: Sat 10am-2pm *Admission:* Free. *Site Info:* Free on-site parking. Wheelchair accessible. Tour guide available.

Exhibits at the Vassar Museum pertain to Vassar High School, the founder of Vassar, Townsend North items, lumbering, and farming. **Information may not be current.*

Watrousville Museum
4607 W. Caro Road (M-81), Vassar, MI 48768 (43.451928, -83.526627)
(989) 823-2360, dave@watrousville.com, www.watrousville.com
Hours: Jun-Sep: Thu 1-4pm. Also by appointment. *Admission:* Free. *Site Info:* Free on-site parking. Not wheelchair accessible. Tour guide available.

The Watrousville Museum is located in the former Watrous General Store, which is listed in the State Register of Historic Sites.

WARREN

Bunert School
27900 Bunert Road, Warren, MI 48092 (42.498404, -82.976523)
(586) 258-2056, warrenhistsoc@yahoo.com, www.warrenhistsoc.org
Hours: 1st Sun monthly 1-4pm (except on holidays and in Feb). *Admission:* Free. Call for group pricing. *Site Info:* On-site parking. Wheelchair accessible. Self-guided. Group tours available by appointment; call for pricing.

In 2012, the Burnet School was listed in the National Register of Historic Places. This restored one-room school features exhibits dating back to 1875-1944.

Warren Historical Gallery at the Warren Community Center
5460 Arden, Warren, MI 48092 (42.529797, -83.053496)
(586) 258-2056, histcomm@cityofwarren.org,
www.cityofwarren.org/index.php/historic-commission,
www.warrenhistsoc.org
Hours: Sep-May: Mon-Fri 9am-5pm. Also by appointment.
Admission: Free. *Site Info:* Tour guide available upon request;
donations accepted.

The Warren Historical Commission, in cooperation with Warren
Historical & Genealogical Society, maintains a historical gallery in
the Warren Community Center. The Warren Historical Gallery's
exhibits encompass pre-1807 "The Impassable Swamp" through the
development of the city. The gallery concludes with "Warren Today
2000-2010."

WASHINGTON

Greater Washington Area Historical Society
58230 Van Dyke, Washington, MI 48094 (42.723107, -83.0355209)
(248) 652-2458, holcomi@comcast.net, www.washhistsoc.org
Hours: Jun-Nov: 2nd and 4th Sun 1-4pm. *Site Info:* Free on-site
parking. Not wheelchair accessible. Self-guided.

The Greater Washington Area Historical Society Museum features
an extensive display on George Washington, a room devoted to
military history, and more. Within the museum is a Boy Scout
Museum, which contains the largest collection of Boy Scout
paraphernalia in Michigan. There are also many items belonging to
the area's early settlers on display.

Loren Andrus Octagon House
57500 VanDyke Ave., Washington, MI 48094 (42.717863,
-83.0355223)
(586) 781-0084, info@octagonhouse.org, www.octagonhouse.org
Hours: By appointment only. *Admission:* $5. *Site Info:* Free on-site
parking. Wheelchair accessible.

The 1860s Loren Andrus Octagon House was inspired by Orson
Squire Fowler's publication "The Octagon House: A Home for All."
It is thought that the house may have been a stop along the
Underground Railroad. It has been used for a variety of different
endeavors, ranging from an inn to the Wayne State Agricultural
program.

WATERFORD

Historic Waterford Village
4490 Hatchery Road, Waterford, MI 48330 (42.675305,

-83.377776)
(248) 683-2697, sstrait649@comcast.net,
www.waterfordhistoricalsociety.org
Hours: Wed 10:30am-2pm. *Admission:* Free. *Site Info:* On-site
parking. Wheelchair accessible. Guided tours.

The early 1900s Historic Waterford Village includes a 1919
Hatchery House, log cabin, Jacober's General Store, Drayton Plains
Depot, Grand Tunk caboose and water tower, carriage house,
millinery, barber shop, hardware store, print shop, doctor and dentist
offices, bakery, and service station.

WAYNE

Wayne Historical Museum
North East Biddle and Main Street, Wayne, MI 48184 (42.281055,
-83.384771)
(734) 722-0113, rstory@ci.wayne.mi.us,
www.ci.wayne.mi.us/historical_museum.shtml
Hours: Fri-Sat 1-4pm. *Admission:* Free. *Site Info:* Lot or street
parking. Wheelchair accessible. Tour guide available.

Located in the former city offices building (c. 1878), the Wayne
Historical Museum opened in 1964 and features more than 100
exhibits tracing the path from village to city.

WEST BLOOMFIELD

Chaldean Cultural Center
5600 Walnut Lake Road, West Bloomfield, MI 48323 (42.557095,
-83.397388)
(248) 681-5050, mromaya@chaldeanculturalcenter.org,
www.chaldeanculturalcenter.org
Hours: Call for hours. *Site Info:* Free on-site parking. Tour guide
available by appointment.

Set to open early 2014, the Chaldean Cultural Center promotes the
history and accomplishments of the Chaldean people and covers
more than 5,000 years of Chaldean history. Artifacts on display
include a Sumerian clay messenger tablet, and exhibits include a
Chaldean-owned grocery store as it would have appeared in 1930s
Detroit.

Jewish Historical Society of Michigan Tours
6600 W. Maple Road, West Bloomfield, MI 48322 (42.543437,
-83.402152)
(248) 432-5517, info@michjewishhistory.org,
www.michjewishhistory.org

Hours: By appointment. *Admission:* Free. *Site Info:* On-site parking. Wheelchair accessible. Tour guide available.

The Jewish Historical Society of Michigan offers several tours that blend the history of the region with the exciting developments of Jewish Detroit and Michigan today. Tour stops include former Jewish neighborhoods, synagogues, historic markers, and significant sites.

WESTLAND

Nankin Mills Interpretive Center

33175 Ann Arbor Trail, Westland, MI 48185 (42.344374, -83.271871)
(724) 261-1850, friends@nankinmills.org; cclement@waynecounty.com, www.nankinmills.org
Hours: Mon-Sat 9am-4pm. *Admission:* Donations accepted. *Site Info:* Free on-site parking. Wheelchair accessible. Tour guide available for groups with a minimum of 10 people; $2/adult and $6/child. To schedule a tour, call (734) 261-1850.

Henry Ford purchased Nankin Mills in 1918 as part of his Village Industry project, during which he converted local waterpower mill sites into small factories to make parts for his growing automobile industry. Today, the site tells this story through historic photos and equipment, including a hydroelectric generator that was installed by Ford and Thomas Edison. Exhibits also consider the history of the Rouge River floodplain, the Three Fires tribes who lived along the Rouge River, and more.

WHITE LAKE

Kelley-Fisk Farm

9180 Highland Road, White Lake, MI 48383 (42.657795, -83.468174)
(248) 887-3244, jozoning@aol.com, www.whitelakehistory.org
Hours: Last Tue monthly. Also by appointment and during special events. *Admission:* Donations accepted. *Site Info:* Free on-site parking. Wheelchair accessible. Tour guide available by appointment; call at least one week in advance.

Operated by the White Lake Historical Society, the Kelley-Fisk Farm features an 1855 farmhouse completely furnished with antiques, 1876 one-room school, turn-of-the-century barn full of farm-related antiques, and a 1930s kitchen display. The original hen house, pig house, pump house, and corn cribs are also on the site.

WYANDOTTE

Ford-MacNichol Home
2610 Biddle Ave., Wyandotte, MI 48192 (42.207444, -83.14891)
(734)324-7284, museum@wyan.org, www.wyandottemuseums.org
Hours: Apr-Dec: Thu-Sun 12-4pm. *Admission:* Adults $5, Children
(5-12) $2.50, Children (4 and under) free. *Site Info:* Free on-site and
street parking. Partially wheelchair accessible; facility does not have
a wheelchair accessible restroom (although there is one in the Marx
Home). Tour guide available; contact museum for group tour
information and pricing.

The Wyandotte Museums' main exhibit building is housed in the
1896 Victorian Ford-MacNichol Home, which features a wraparound porch, tower, six fireplaces, original oak woodwork, period
decor, and exhibits highlighting local history. Seasonal exhibits and
period vignettes feature the organization's collections.

YPSILANTI

Ypsilanti Automotive Heritage Museum
100 E. Cross St., Ypsilanti, MI 48198 (42.245859, -83.608056)
(734) 482-5200, hudsondealer@ypsiautoheritage.org,
www.ypsiautoheritage.org
Hours: Tue-Sun 1-5pm. *Admission:* Adults $5, Children (0-12) free.
Site Info: On-site parking. Wheelchair accessible. Self-guided.

Located in the world's last operating Hudson auto dealership
building, the Ypsilanti Automotive Heritage Museum is dedicated to
Ypsilanti's auto history. The museum houses records dating back to
1927 and displays 30 vehicles and 18 cutaway automatic
transmissions.

Ypsilanti Historical Society, Museum, & Archives
220 N. Huron St., Ypsilanti, MI 48197 (42.244701, -83.612679)
(734) 482-4990, yhs.museum@gmail.com,
www.ypsilantihistoricalsociety.org
Hours: Tue-Sun 2-5pm. *Admission:* Free. *Site Info:* Free on-site
parking. Wheelchair accessible. Tour guide available by
appointment; $1/person for large groups.

The Ypsilanti Historical Society's museum is located in the Asa
Dow House, an 1860s brick Victorian mansion. On display are
artifacts from the 19th and 20th centuries and exhibits depicting
Ypsilanti's heritage.

NORTHERN

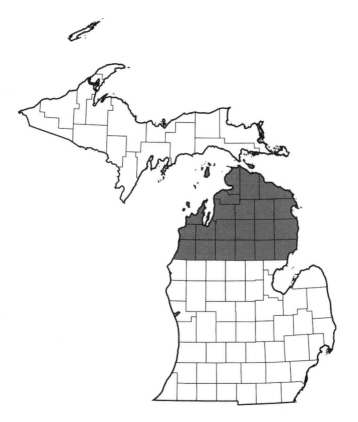

ACME

Music House Museum

7377 U.S. 31 N, Acme, MI 49610 (44.792758, -85.487869)
(231) 938-9300, info@musichouse.org, www.musichouse.org
Hours: May-Oct: Mon-Sat 10am-4pm, Sun 12pm-4pm; Nov-Dec:
Sat 10am-4pm; Dec 26-31: Daily 10am-4pm. *Admission:* Adults
$11, Youth (6-15) $4, Family $25. *Site Info:* On-site parking.
Wheelchair accessible. Guided tours.

The Music House Museum collects, restores, and preserves
automated music machines and instruments from the 1870s to the
1930s. Guided tours explain and demonstrate the unique
instruments, which include a Belgian dance organ, nickelodeons,
music boxes, pipe organs, and Wurlitzer Theater Organ. The
museum also features a scale model of Traverse City (c. 1930).
* Information may not be current.

ALPENA

Besser Museum for Northeast Michigan
491 Johnson St., Alpena, MI 49707 (45.079934, -83.446029)
(989) 356-2202, adozier@bessermuseum.org,
www.bessermuseum.org
Hours: Mon-Sat 10am-5pm. *Admission:* Adults $5, Seniors and
Children $3. *Site Info:* On-site parking. Wheelchair accessible. Self-
guided.

The Besser Museum for Northeast Michigan hosts four permanent
and five rotating exhibits featuring Native American artifacts,
Alpena's history, nature history, and more. The "Avenue of Shops"
gallery represents stores and businesses in Alpena during the 1890s.
Visitors can also explore the site's five historic buildings, which
include the 1872 Maltz Exchange Bank and 1863 Lousada
Homestead Cabin.

Great Lakes Maritime Heritage Center
500 W. Fletcher St., Alpena, MI 49707 (45.067278, -83.433002)
(989) 356-8805, (989) 354-0144, thunderbay@noaa.gov,
www.thunderbay.noaa.gov
Hours: See website. *Admission:* Free. *Site Info:* Free on-site and
street parking. Wheelchair accessible. Self-guided.

Located in Lake Huron, Thunder Bay is adjacent to one of the most
treacherous stretches of water within the Great Lakes, earning the
area the name "Shipwreck Alley." Today, the 448-square-mile
Thunder Bay National Marine Sanctuary protects one of America's
best-preserved collections of more than 200 shipwrecks. The
sanctuary's visitors center, the Great Lakes Maritime Heritage
Center, features 11,000 square feet of exhibits, including a life-size
replica of a Great Lakes schooner battling a storm and a shipwreck.

ARCADIA

Arcadia Area Historical Museum
3340 Lake St., Arcadia, MI 49613 (44.493469, -86.235246)
(231) 889-4360, www.arcadiami.com
Hours: Thu-Sat 1-4pm, Sun 1-3pm. Also by appointment; call Joyce
at (231) 889-3389. *Admission:* Free. *Site Info:* Free on-site parking.
Wheelchair accessible. Tour guide available.

The Arcadia Area Historical Museum is located in a Victorian house
built in 1884 by an early settler named Howard Gilbert. Exhibits tell
the story of the Arcadia Furniture Company, the Arcadia & Betsey
River Railway, the Arcadia Channel, the sunken *Minnehaha*, area
baseball, and Harriet Quimby ("America's First Lady in the Air").

ATLANTA

McKenzie One-Room School
13110 M-33 N, Atlanta, MI 49709 (45.029862, -84.163856)
(989) 742-4218
Hours: 3rd week in Aug 10am-9pm. *Admission:* Fair entry fee. *Site Info:* Fairground parking; small fee during the week of the fair. Wheelchair accessible.

Located in the Montmorency County Fair Grounds, the McKenzie One-Room School is operated by the Montmorency County Historical Society.

BELLAIRE

Bellaire Historical Museum
202 N. Bridge St., Bellaire, MI 49615 (44.976759, -85.209617)
(231) 533-8631, bellairemuseum1@gmail.com
Hours: Tue-Sat 11am-3pm. *Admission:* Free. *Site Info:* Free street parking. Wheelchair accessible. Tour guide available.

The Bellaire Historical Museum features Civil War uniforms and weapons, a pioneer cabin, the history of Bellaire High School, and the story of the world's largest wooden ware factory.

CADILLAC

Wexford County Historical Society Museum
127 Beech St., Cadillac, MI 49601 (44.251003, -85.399966)
(231) 775-1717, info@wexfordcountyhistory.org,
www.wexfordcountyhistory.org
Hours: See website. *Admission:* Adults $3, Family $5, Children (0-15) free. *Site Info:* Street parking. Not wheelchair accessible. Free. Tour guide available.

Located in a former Carnegie library, the Wexford County Historical Society Museum is the leading source of displays relating to the history of Wexford County. The 5,000-square-foot museum contains artifacts, photographs, maps, paintings, documents, and exhibits that reflect the community's history since its inception in the 1870s. Displays include military exhibits (WWI, WWII, Korean, and Vietnam), tools of trade, a medical office, a general store, and Native American artifacts.

CHARLEVOIX

Castle Farms
5052 M-66, Charlevoix, MI 49720 (45.277622, -85.226858)

(231) 237-0884, *peggy@castlefarms.com, www.castlefarms.com*
Hours: May 1-Oct 31: Daily 9:30am-4pm. Call ahead to verify
hours. *Admission:* Adults $9, Seniors (65+) $8, Children (2-12) $5.
Site Info: Wheelchair accessible. Guided group tours available by
appointment; call (231) 237-0884, ext. 224. See website for optional
tour add-ons, including lawn games and educational services.

Built in 1918, Castle Farms was once the home of Albert Loeb and
his prize-winning herd of Holstein-Friesian dairy cows. On display
are posters, music scores, uniforms, and other memorabilia from the
Great War era. From May to October, guests can also watch one of
the state's largest working model garden railroads, where 55 G-scale
trains operate on more than 2,000 feet of track.

Charlevoix Depot
307 Chicago Ave., Charlevoix, MI 49720 (45.318453, -85.244546)
(231) 547-0373, chxhistory@sbcglobal.net, www.chxhistory.com
Hours: By appointment. *Admission:* Donations accepted. *Site Info:*
Free on-site and street parking. Wheelchair accessible. Self-guided.

Built by the Chicago & West Michigan Railway in 1892, the
Charlevoix Depot is used for meetings, events, and occasional
exhibits. The depot is listed in the National Historic Register of
Historic Places and the interior may be viewed upon request. On the
exterior, the Charlevoix Area Garden Club has developed an award-
winning Heritage Garden using historic cuttings and design
methods. This area is open to the public at all times.

Harsha House Museum
103 State St., Charlevoix, MI 49720 (45.317670, -85.261116)
(231) 547-0373, chxhistory@sbcglobal.net, www.chxhistory.com
Hours: Call for hours. *Admission:* $1 suggested donation. *Site Info:*
Free on-site and street parking. Wheelchair accessible. Tour guide
available.

Built in 1891 by Charlevoix businessman Horace Harsha, the
Harsha House Museum includes three restored Victorian parlors
with vintage furnishings and original artwork by Charlevoix artists.
One highlight is Ernest Hemingway's original marriage license with
first wife, Hadley Richardson, the "Paris Wife." Other attractions
include a working player piano that may be played by the public
under supervision, a 3 1/2 Order Fresnel lens from the Gray's Reef
light north of Beaver Island, and more.

CHEBOYGAN

Cheboygan County History Center
427 Court St., Cheboygan, MI 49721 (45.639462, -84.483785)

(616) 627-9597, lcrusoe@cheboyganhistorycenter.org,
www.cheboyganhistorycenter.org
Hours: Jun-Sep: Tue-Sat 1-4pm. *Admission:* Adults $5, Children
free. *Site Info:* On-site parking. Partially wheelchair accessible;
some buildings require stairway access. Tour guide available.

Three separate buildings make up Cheboygan County History
Center. Spies Heritage Hall houses the center's principal exhibits,
which consider the Native American presence in the Straits area, the
military service of local residents, the county's maritime industries
and activities, and Cheboygan's participation in the lumbering
industry. Built in the 1880s, the Sheriff's Residence and Jail contains
period settings of life in the 1880s and early 1900s. The mid-1800s
log cabin depicts Native American life in the early 1900s.

Cheboygan River Front Light
606 Water St., Cheboygan, MI 49721 (45.647311, -84.472723)
(231) 436-5580, info@gllka.com, www.gllka.com
Hours: Memorial Day to Labor Day: Weekends and Holidays 9am-
5pm. *Admission:* Donations accepted. *Site Info:* Free on-site
parking. Not wheelchair accessible. Tour guide available.

Under the stewardship of the Great Lakes Lighthouse Keepers
Association, the Cheboygan River Front Light is in the midst of a
restoration project. The light will return to its appearance in 1910,
when Cheboygan was in its heyday. Volunteer keepers can provide
tours for visitors.

COPEMISH

Marilla Museum & Pioneer Place
9991 Marilla Road, Copemish, MI 496 5   44. 815   , -85.87919
(231) 362-3430, boja@kaltelnet.net, www.marillahistory.org
Hours: May-Oct: Last Sat monthly 1-5pm. Also by appointment.
Admission: Adults $3, Children (8+) $1.50 *Site Info:* Free on-site
parking. Partially wheelchair accessible. Tour guide available.

The grounds of the Marilla Museum and Pioneer Place include the
two-story log Pioneer House, the Nels Johnson Cabin, and the fully
furnished 1900 Pioneer Barn. The 1920 Standard School, which also
serves as the Marilla Township Hall, contains two large museum
spaces.

EAST JORDAN

East Jordan Portside Art & Historical Museum
01656 S. M-66, East Jordan, MI 49727 (45.229319, -85.181711)
(231) 536-3282, kprebble@ejps.org, www.portsideartsfair.org
Hours: Jun-Sep: Sat-Sun afternoons. Also by appointment; call at

least 24 hours in advance. *Admission:* Donations accepted. *Site Info:* Free on-site parking. Wheelchair accessible. Tour guide available.

The East Jordan Portside Art & Historical Museum is located in Elm Pointe Park, a Michigan Historic Site located on Lake Charlevoix. The seasonal museum includes military uniforms and memorabilia; railroad, lumbering, and local manufacturing; medical doctor and veterinary instruments; and more.

EAST TAWAS

Tawas Point Lighthouse
686 Tawas Beach Road, East Tawas, MI 48730 (44.253368, -83.446762)
(989) 362-5658, museuminfo@michigan.gov,
www.michigan.gov/tawaslighthouse
Hours: See website. *Admission:* $2. Also, a Michigan State Parks Recreation Passport is required for entry. *Site Info:* Free on-site parking. Information can be provided in Braille if staff is given advance notice. Tour guide available.

In operation since 1876, the Tawas Point Lighthouse is part of Tawas Point State Park. There are other historic structures on site, including an oil house and a fog signal area.

ELK RAPIDS

Elk Rapids Area Historical Museum
301 Traverse St., Elk Rapids, MI 48629 (44.896585,-85.415636)
(231) 264-5692, president@elkrapidshistory.org,
www.elkrapidshistory.org
Hours: Memorial Day to Sep: Fri-Sat 10am-4pm, Sun 1-4pm.
Admission: Donations accepted. *Site Info:* Free street parking. Partially wheelchair accessible. Tour guide available. For group tours during open hours, call (231) 264-5692; for group tours after hours, call (231) 264-8984.

Exhibits and displays at the Elk Rapids Area Historical Museum focus on Elk Rapids' role in the "Chain of Lakes Region" during the 19th and 20th centuries as an important lumbering, cement, and pig iron smelting center.

EMPIRE

Empire Area Museum Complex
11544 S. LaCore St., Empire, MI 49630 (44.819288, -86.058394)
(231) 326-5568, empiremuseum@centurytel.net,
www.leelanau.cc/government0293.asp
Hours: Memorial Day to July 1: Sat-Sun 1-4pm; Jul-Aug: Thu-Tue

1-4pm; Labor Day to Oct: Sat-Sun 1-4pm. *Admission:* Suggested donation $2/person. *Site Info:* Free on-site parking. Wheelchair accessible. Self-guided. Heritage Day (Oct).

The main building at the Empire Area Museum Complex houses "Roen Saloon," Empire's turn-of-the-century saloon with all the fixtures; Empire's 19 4 gas station; and more. The Billy Beeman Barn contains horse-drawn equipment and other farming related items. The third building is a turn-of-the-century one-room school combined with a church. And the relocated Hose House, or firehouse, features early "hand pulled" firefighting equipment.

FIFE LAKE

Fife Lake Historical Museum
136 E. State St., Fife Lake, MI 49633 (44.576594, -85.349848)
(231) 879-3342, www.fifelake.com/chamber/historical.htm
Hours: Memorial Day to Labor Day. Call for hours. *Admission:* Free. *Site Info:* On-site parking. Wheelchair accessible. Tour guide available.

The Fife Lake Historical Museum is full of numerous historical artifacts and displays relating to the history of the village. While at the museum, visitors can also pick up a brochure/map for the historic walking tour, which includes the authentic brick Fife Lake Hardware, historic fire barn, and more.

FRANKFORT

Point Betsie Lighthouse
3071 Point Betsie Road, Frankfort, MI 49635 (44.691268, -86.255196)
(231) 352-7644, info@pointbetsie.org, www.pointbetsie.org
Hours: Memorial Day to Labor Day: Sat 10:30am-4:30pm, Sun 12:30-4:30pm; Jul-Aug: Fri 10:30am-4:30pm. *Admission:* Adults $4, Children (6-11) $2, Children (0-5) free. *Site Info:* Street parking at end of Point Betsie Road. Wheelchair accessible. Tour guide available.

The Point Betsie Lighthouse remains an official navigational aid maintained by the U.S. Coast Guard. Extensive displays cover lightkeeping and lifesaving at Point Betsie. Attractions include the century-old Fourth Order Fresnel lens.
Information may not be current.

GAYLORD

Otsego County Historical Museum
320 W. Main St., Gaylord, MI 49734 (45.027212, -84.678835)

(989) 732-4568, ochsmuseum@gmail.com, www.otsego.org/ochs
Hours: Mon-Tue and Thu-Sat 11am-5pm. *Admission:* Free. *Site Info:* On-site parking. Wheelchair accessible. Self-guided.

The Otsego County Historical Museum is located in a former cigar factory building (c. 1911). Exhibits highlight lumbering, farming, furniture, commerce, and the Dayton Lost Block Works of Gaylord.

GRAYLING

Crawford County Historical Society & Museum Complex
97 E. Michigan Ave., Grayling, MI 49738 (44.668799, -84.707945)
(989) 348-4461, cchs49738@yahoo.com, www.grayling-area.com/museum
Hours: 12-4pm. *Admission:* Donations accepted. *Site Info:* Free street parking. Partially wheelchair accessible; first floor only. Tour guide available upon request.

The Crawford County Historical Society maintains a museum complex that includes an 1882 train depot, a 1900 schoolhouse that features the county's military history, authentic log trapper's cabin, and more. Displays look at the history of the AuSable River, the AuSable Canoe Marathon since 1947, law enforcement, etc.

Hartwick Pines Logging Museum
4216 Ranger Road, Grayling, MI 49738 (44.744881, -84.648005)
(989) 348-2537, burgr@michigan.gov,
www.michigan.gov/loggingmuseum
Hours: May 1-24: Daily 9am-4pm; May 25-Sep 2: Daily 10am-6pm; Sep 3-Oct 31: Daily 9am-4pm. *Admission:* Free, although a Michigan State Parks Recreation Passport is required for entry. *Site Info:* Free on-site parking. Partially wheelchair accessible. Self-guided.

Hartwick Pines Logging Museum is situated among the towering trees of one of Michigan's largest remaining stands of old-growth white pine. The exhibits return visitors to the state's 19th-century logging era, when Michigan led the nation in sawed lumber production. The visitor center, logging camp, exhibits, and period rooms tell the stories of the loggers, river men, and entrepreneurs who powered Michigan's white pine industry.

Lovells Township Historical Society Museum
Lovells Museum of Trout Fishing History
8405 Twin Bridge Road, Grayling, MI 49738 (44.805101, -84.485014)
(989) 348-7173, lovellsmuseum@yahoo.com,
www.lovellsmuseum.com

Hours: May-Sep: Wed and Fri-Sun 10am-4pm. *Admission:* Donations accepted. *Site Info:* Tour guide available.

The Lovells Township Historical Society maintains two museum buildings. The 1907 Lone Pine School House houses Lovells Township Historical Society Museum, which shares Lovells' community history. Built adjacent to the school building is the Lovells Museum of Trout Fishing History, which shares the history of the AuSable River.
Information may not be current.

Wellington Farm Park
6944 S. Military Road, Grayling, MI 49738 (44.583865, -84.770851)
(989) 529-7331, welfar32@gmail.com,
www.wellingtonfarmpark.org
Hours: Jun-Oct: Daily 9am-5pm. *Admission:* Adults $7.50, Seniors and Students $5.50. *Site Info:* Free on-site parking. Wheelchair accessible. Tour guide available.

Wellington Farm is a 60-acre living history farm, dedicated to the preservation of life as it was lived in a Midwestern farming community during the Great Depression. Buildings include a blacksmith shop, broom shop, sawmill, and more—all fully functional and often manned and in operation by interpreters in period costume. In 2013, the farm opened an ice cream shop selling homemade ice cream frozen with ice and salt in an old-fashioned freezer that is powered by a 1920 John Deere engine.

HARBOR SPRINGS

Andrew J. Blackbird Museum
368 Main St., Harbor Springs, MI 49740 (45.430422, -84.984752)
(2320 526-0612,
*www.visitharborspringsmichigan.com/stories/andrew_j_blackbird_*
museum_harbor_springs

The son of an Ottawa chief, Andrew J. Blackbird was born in what is now Harbor Springs around 1815. He helped Native American veterans receive pensions, settle land claims, and secure citizenship. His house now serves as the Andrew J. Blackbird Museum, which is filled with Native American artifacts.
Information may not be current.

Harbor Springs History Museum
349 E. Main St., Harbor Springs, MI 49740 (45.430639, -84.985316)
(231) 526-9771, info@harborspringshistory.org,
www.harborspringshistory.org
Hours: Call or see website. *Admission:* Adults $5, Seniors and

Children $3. *Site Info:* Free on-site and street parking. Wheelchair accessible. Self-guided.

Housed in the former city hall building (b. 1886), the Harbor Springs History Museum features exhibits with hands-on activities for kids of all ages. The permanent exhibit galleries detail the unique history of the Harbor Springs area and the temporary exhibit space changes on an annual basis to feature a variety of topics of both local and statewide interest.

HARRISVILLE

Sturgeon Point Lighthouse
Old Bailey School
6072 E. Point Road, Harrisville, MI 48470 (44.710827, -83.27265)
(989) 727-4703, lklemens@ymail.com,
www.alconahistoricalsociety.com
Hours: Jun-Sep: 11am-4pm. *Admission:* Free. *Site Info:* Free on-site parking. Partially wheelchair accessible; grounds and gift shop only. Self-guided.

The Sturgeon Point Lighthouse features an authentic lens, keeper's home with all rooms restored and furnished, and two old boats used by Coast Guard of the era. Also on site is an Alcona County one-room schoolhouse, completely restored and furnished with authentic collections.

Lincoln Train Depot
Lake Street and Fisk Street, Lincoln, MI 48742 (44.6837692, -83.4134094)
(989) 727-4703, lklemens@ymail.com,
www.alconahistoricalsociety.com
Hours: Call or e-mail. *Admission:* Free. *Site Info:* Free on-site parking. Wheelchair accessible. Self-guided.

Standing since 1886, the wooden Lincoln Train Depot was built by the Detroit, Bay City and Alpena Railroad and served the community until 1929. It the last remaining train depot of its kind in Northeast Michigan and is listed in the State Register of Historic Sites. The display includes an actual caboose and switching engine.

HILLMAN

Brush Creek Mill
121 State St., Hillman, MI 49746 (45.0632722, -83.901375)
(989) 742-2527, brushcreekmill@myfrontiermail.com,
www.brushcreekmill.com
Hours: Jan-Apr: Fri-Sat 12-4pm; May-Dec: Tue-Sat 12-4pm.

Admission: Free. *Site Info:* On-site parking. Wheelchair accessible. Tour guide available by appointment.

Located on the property of a former gristmill, the Brush Creek Mill features the history of local families as well as information pertaining to solar power, water power, wind turbines, and geo-thermal energy. The Hillman Historical Society shares the site and helps with the changing displays.

HOUGHTON LAKE

Houghton Lake Area Historical Village

1701 W. Houghton Lake Drive, Houghton Lake, MI 48629 (44.298651, -84.719084)
(989) 422-6393, chuckandag@charter.net,
www.houghtonlakehistory.com
Hours: Summer: Fri-Sat 12-4pm. Also by appointment. *Admission:* $3. *Site Info:* Free on-site parking. Wheelchair accessible. Tour guide available.

The 13-building Houghton Lake Area Historical Village replicates a 19th-century logging-era community. The site includes the *Edna Times* print shop, an original hand-hewn log school house, and an operating general store. The adjacent historical playhouse was built in 1927 as the Johnson Dance Hall.

KALEVA

Bottle House Museum

14551 Wuoksi St., Kaleva, MI 49645 (44.373228, -86.009345)
(231) 362-2080, caasiala@jackpine.com, Find on Facebook
Hours: Memorial Day to Labor Day: Sat-Sun 12-4pm; Sep-Oct: Sat 12-4pm. *Admission:* $3 suggested donation. *Site Info:* Street parking; also church parking lot. Not wheelchair accessible. Tour guide availability and cost vary.

The historic Bottle House Museum was built in 1942 by John Makinen using 60,000 soda pop bottles from his bottle factory. Displays interpret Kaleva history.

Railroad Depot Museum

14420 Walta St., Kaleva, MI 49645 (44.3749715, -86.011759)
(231) 362-2080, caasiala@jackpine.com, www.kalevami.com;
www.allartsmanistee.com
Hours: Memorial Day to Labor Day: Sat 12-4pm. *Admission:* Donations accepted. *Site Info:* On-site parking. Wheelchair accessible. Tour guide availability and cost vary.

The Railroad Depot Museum features railroad memorabilia and an M+NE engine.

LAKE ANN

Almira Historical Society Museum

19440 Maple St., Lake Ann, MI 49650 (44.723792, -85.847610)
(231) 275-7362, info@almirahistoricalsociety.org,
www.almirahistoricalsociety.org
Hours: Memorial Day to Labor Day: Tue and Sat 1-4pm. Also by appointment. *Admission:* Free. *Site Info:* Free parking. Wheelchair accessible. Tour guide available.

The Almira Historical Society Museum has more than 1,300 artifacts and includes the Thompson-Kuemin House, which has been restored to the 1940s era. The property also includes the Almira Fire Barn Museum, which houses a 1946 International fire truck. There is also a blacksmith shop and boathouse. The Babcock House is currently being restored to the late-1800s era.

LELAND

Historic Fishtown

199 to 205 W. River St., Leland, MI 49654 (45.023840, -85.761898)
(231) 256-8878, info@fishtownmi.org, www.fishtownmi.org
Site Info: Free street parking. Limited wheelchair accessibility. Group tours available by appointment.

Located in Leland, Historic Fishtown's attractions include historic fishing shanties, regional foods, unique shops, and exhibits about Fishtown's past and present as a working waterfront. Some exhibits are viewable all year; others are seasonal.

Leelanau Historical Society and Museum

203 E. Cedar St., Leland, MI 49654 (45.022149, -85.762060)
(231) 256-7475, info@leelanauhistory.org,
www.leelanauhistory.org
Hours: Wed-Fri 10am-4pm, Sat 10am-2pm. Also by chance or appointment on Tuesday. *Admission:* Free. *Site Info:* Free on-site parking. Wheelchair accessible. Self-guided.

The Leelanau Historical Society and Museum preserves and displays the history of the the Leelanau Peninsula and its islands. Its exhibits include the shipwrecks of the Manitou Passage, North Manitou Island, and the Native American Anishnabek Arts Collection.

LEWISTON

Kneeland-Sachs Museum

4384 Michelson Ave., Lewiston, MI 49756 (44.885230, -84.305086)
(989) 786-2451, lewareahistsoc@gmail.com
Hours: Summer: Sat. Also by appointment. *Admission:* Donations
accepted. *Site Info:* Free on-site parking. Partially wheelchair
accessible. Tour guide available during open hours or by
appointment.

Built in 1892, the Kneeland-Sachs Museum was previously the
home of David Kneeland, manager of the Michelson & Hanson
Lumber Company, and later George and Martha Sachs. The museum
shares the histories of both of these families. Maintained by the
Lewiston Area Historical Society, the site also features a fully
furnished trapper's cabin as well as a barn housing an extensive
collection of lumbering equipment.

Lunden Civilian Conservation Corps Camp

North Side of County Road 612, Lewiston, MI 49676 (44.884170,
-84.17939)
(989) 786-2451, lewareahistsoc@gmail.com
Admission: Free. *Site Info:* Free on-site parking. Wheelchair
accessible. Self-guided.

Established in June 1933, Camp Lunden was one of 103 Michigan
Civilian Conservation Corps camps that planted trees; built roads,
fire lines, and trout ponds; and cleared the air field for the Atlanta
airport. The camp closed in 1936 and is listed in the State Register
of Historic Sites. Today, the site features a display of photos and
documents related to the camp.

MACKINAW CITY

Colonial Michilimackinac

102 W. Straits Ave., Mackinaw City, MI 49701 (45.787936,
-84.732327)
(231) 436-4100, mackinacparks@michigan.gov,
www.mackinacparks.com
Hours: Early May to mid-Oct: 9:30am-5pm; peak summer season
hours extended to 7pm. *Admission:* Adults $11, Youth (5-17) $6.50.
Site Info: On-site parking. Partially wheelchair accessible; see
"Guide to Access" brochure available at sites. Costumed interpretive
guides daily.

The French fur-trading village and military outpost Michilimackinac
was founded in 1715. It was later occupied by the British, who
abandoned it in 1780 to establish a new fort on Mackinac Island.
Today, the site features a reconstructed fortified village of 13

buildings as it appeared in the 1770s, based on evidence gathered during the nation's longest archaeological excavation.

Heritage Village

1425 West Central Ave., Mackinaw City, MI 49701 (45.781501, -84.769113)
(231) 373-9793, mail@mackinawhistory.org,
www.mackinawhistory.com
Hours: See website. *Admission:* Free. *Site Info:* Free on-site parking. Partially wheelchair accessible. Tour guide available Memorial Day to Labor Day: Sat-Mon 1-4pm.

Operated by the Mackinaw Area Historical Society, Heritage Village educates visitors about the era of 1880-1917 as it was experienced by residents of the Mackinaw City area. The village includes the Pestilence House, a church, an artifacts building, a sawmill that cut the timbers for the Soo Locks, a one-room schoolhouse, a log cabin, the Stimpson Homestead, a machine shed, a tar paper shack, and wigwams.

Historic Mill Creek Discovery Park

9001 US-23, Mackinaw City, MI 49701 (45.743703, -84.668154)
(231) 436-4100, mackinacparks@michigan.gov,
www.mackinacparks.com
Hours: Early May to mid-Oct: 9am-4:30pm; peak summer season hours extended to 5:30pm. *Admission:* Adults $8, Youth (5-17) $4.75. *Site Info:* On-site parking. Partially wheelchair accessible; see "Guide to Access" brochure available at sites. Costumed interpretive guides daily.

The Straits' first industrial complex, now the site of the Historic Mill Creek Discovery Park, provided lumber for the settlement of Mackinac Island in the 1790s. Attractions include demonstrations of hand-saw techniques and a reconstructed 18th-century water-driven sawmill. There are also natural history programs, nature trails, and daily "high ropes" adventure tours.

Old Mackinac Point Lighthouse

526 N. Huron Ave., Mackinaw City, MI 49701 (45.787524, -84.729437)
(231) 436-4100, mackinacparks@michigan.gov,
www.mackinacparks.com
Hours: Early May to mid-Oct: 9am-4:30pm; peak summer season, hours extended to 5:30pm. *Admission:* Adults $6.50, Youth (5-17) $4. *Site Info:* On-site parking. Partially wheelchair accessible; see "Guide to Access" brochure available at sites. Costumed interpretive guides daily.

Erected in 1892, the Old Mackinac Point Lighthouse served more than 60 years. The castle-like structure has since been restored to its

1910 appearance and features period settings and hands-on exhibits. Interpreters lead tours up the tower and in the lantern room.

MANCELONA

Mancelona Historical Society

9826 S. Williams, Mancelona, MI 49659 (44.890250, -85.073790)
(231) 587-9687, www.ole.net/~maggie/antrim/mancy.htm
Hours: Jun-Sep: Sat 1-4pm. *Admission:* Donations accepted. *Site Info:* On-site parking. Wheelchair accessible. Tour guide available.

Located in the former Antrim Ceramic Store, the Mancelona Area Historical Society features an Antrim Iron Works exhibit.

MAPLE CITY

Olsen House History Center

3164 W. Harbor Hwy., Maple City, MI 49664 (44.936446, -85.940958)
(231) 334-6103, phsb@leelanau.com, www.phsb.org
Hours: See website. *Admission:* A National Park Pass is required for admission. *Site Info:* Free on-site parking. Wheelchair accessible. Tour guide available.

The office of Preserve Historic Sleeping Bear is located in the Charles and Hattie Olsen Farmhouse in the Port Oneida Rural Historic District. The rehabilitated pioneer homestead shares the history of the Olsen family, the Port Oneida community, and the effect of the National Park on the landscape. The organization also offers a hiking tour/map that takes visitors through the Port Oneida Rural Historic District.

MILLERSBURG

Millersburg Area Historical Society

324 E. Luce St., Millersburg, MI 49759 (45.334615, -84.060993)
(989) 733-8404
Hours: By appointment. *Admission:* Free. *Site Info:* Free on-site parking. Wheelchair accessible. Tour guide available.

The Millersburg Area Historical Society preserves and celebrates the significance of the D&M Railroad Depot as the main means of transportation and communication in the early 20th century. The society showcases artifacts from the area in the only depot remaining in Presque Isle County.
Information may not be current.

NORTHPORT

Grand Traverse Lighthouse Museum

15550 N. Lighthouse Point Road, Northport, MI 49670 (45.210184, -85.549987)

(231) 386-7195, gtlthse@triton.net,
www.grandtraverselighthouse.com
Hours: May: Daily 12-4pm; June-Sep: Daily 10am-5pm; Nov-Dec: Sat-Sun 12-4 pm. *Admission:* Adults $4, Students (6-18) $2. Also, a Michigan State Parks Recreation Passport is required for entry. *Site Info:* Partially wheelchair accessible.

Organized in 1985, the Grand Traverse Lighthouse Museum is located in a 155-year-old lighthouse that has been restored to resemble a keeper's home from the 1920s and 1930s. Exhibits look at area shipwrecks and local history. A restored air diaphone foghorn is demonstrated throughout the year. There is also a fog signal building and oil house on site. Visitors can climb the tower.

OLD MISSION

Hessler Log Cabin

Lighthouse Park, Old Mission, MI 49673 (44.991117, -85.479461)
(231) 947-0947, dobrum@aol.com, www.omphistoricalsociety.org
Hours: Open May to Oct. *Admission:* Free. *Site Info:* Free on-site parking. Wheelchair accessible. Self-guided.

A motion-activated sensor sets off an audio history presentation at the Hessler Log Cabin.

OMENA

Putnam-Cloud Tower House

5045 N. West Bayshore Drive, Omena, MI 49674 (45.055778, -85.588074)

(231) 271-6403, dlystra@sbcglobal.net,
www.omenahistoricalsociety.com
Hours: Jun-Aug: Sat-Sun 1-4pm; Sep-Oct: Sat 1-4pm. *Admission:* Donations accepted. *Site Info:* Free street parking. Not wheelchair accessible. Tour guide available.

The Putnam-Cloud Tower House includes models of Omena's buildings from 1910-20, a reproduction of an 1800s farm kitchen, artifacts including Native American baskets, and books by Omena authors.

OSCODA

Wurtsmith Air Museum

4071 E. Van Ettan, Oscoda, MI 48750 (44.458217, -83.357006)
(989) 739-7555, www.wurtsmithairmusum.org
Hours: Mid-May to Labor Day: Fri-Sun 11am-3pm. *Admission:*
Adults $5, Youth (6-11) $3, Children (0-5) free. *Site Info:* Free
parking. Wheelchair accessible. Tour guide available.

The Wurtsmith Air Museum is located in three fighter-alert hangars
on the former Wurtsmith Air Force Base. On display are aviation
artifacts dating from before the Wright Brothers through the present
day. There is a special emphasis on the military units that were
based at Wurtsmith, beginning with its days as Camp Skeel in the
1920s. Several historic aircraft are under restoration, including a
Cessna O-1A Bird Dog, two T-33As, a Bell UH-1H helicopter, a
Waco, and a CG-4A troop glider.

PESHAWBESTOWN

Eyaawing Museum and Cultural Center

2605 N. West Bay Shore Drive, Peshawbestown, MI 49682
(45.014886, -85.608527)
*(231) 534-7764, museum@gtbindians.com,
www.gtbindians.org/eyaawing.asp*
Hours: Wed-Sat 10am-4pm.

Created by the Grand Traverse Band of Ottawa and Chippewa
Indians, the Eyaawing Museum and Cultural Center establishes,
gathers, interprets, and maintains a record of the history of the
Grand Traverse Band of Anishinaabek with respect for the circle of
life, honor for their families, and the telling of their true heritage.

PETOSKEY

Bay View Historical Museum

1715 Encampment, Petoskey, MI 49770 (45.383793, -84.935076)
*(231) 347-6225, john@bayviewassociation.org,
www.bayviewassociation.org*
Hours: Jun-Aug: Sun 11am-1pm, Mon and Wed 1-3pm. *Admission:*
Free. *Site Info:* Free street parking. Self-guided.

Founded in 1875, Bay View is a historic Chautauqua that was
designated as a National Historic Landmark in 1987. The site has
447 cottages (many considered to be the finest examples of Queen
Anne architecture in the United States). The two oldest buildings on
campus—the Speaker's Stand and the Bookstore—house the Bay
View Historical Museum, which reflects the community's history
and heritage. A new exhibit is featured each summer.

ROGERS CITY

40 Mile Point Lighthouse

7323 U.S. 23 N, Rogers City, MI 48779 (45.490073, -83.927993)
(989) 734-4587, barbara71@hughes.net,
www.40milepointlighthouse.org
Hours: Tue-Sat 10am-4pm, Sun 12-4pm. *Admission:* Free. *Site Info:*
Free on-site parking. Partially wheelchair accessible; grounds and
fog signal building can be accessed via wheelchair. Volunteer guest
lighthouse keepers available for tours during open hours.

The 40 Mile Point Lighthouse Society is dedicated to the restoration
and preservation of 40 Mile Point Lighthouse, complementary
buildings, and the Calcite Pilot House. Also on site is a fog signal
building that has many nautical-themed displays. The society also
offers a guest lighthouse keeper program; see website or call for
more details.

Glawe School Museum

7323 U.S. 23 N, Rogers City, MI 48779 (45.490073, -83.927993)
(989) 733-8659, www.40milepointlighthouse.org
Hours: Memorial Day to late Aug: Sat-Sun 1-4pm. *Admission:*
Donations accepted. *Site Info:* Free on-site parking. Not wheelchair
accessible. Docents available during open hours.

The Glawe School Museum is arranged as a one-room school,
complete with blackboards, student/teacher desks, and piano. While
the museum is located in the 40 Mile Lighthouse Society Park, it is a
separate entity with its own exhibits and budget.

Great Lakes Lore Maritime Museum

367 N. Third St., Rogers City, MI 49779 (45.422690, -83.819540)
(989) 734-0706, www.gllmm.com
Hours: May 1-Dec 1: Mon-Sat 11am-4pm, Sun 11am-3pm; Winter:
Mon 10am-4pm. Also by appointment. *Admission:* Adults $3,
Children (0-11) free. *Site Info:* On-site parking. Wheelchair
accessible.

The Great Lakes Lore Maritime Museum preserves the history of
Great Lakes shipping and the people who worked the lakes.There is
a large display of ship models, photographs, and artifacts. The
Memorial Hall honors the crews of the *Carl D. Bradley*, S.S.
Cedarville, *Daniel J. Morrell*, and *Edmund Fitzgerald.*

Henry and Margaret Hoffman Annex

185 W. Michigan Ave., Rogers City, MI 49779 (45.419984,

-83.817840)
(989) 734-0123, bradleymuseum@yahoo.com,
www.thebradleyhouse.org
Hours: May-Dec: Wed-Sun 12:30-4:30pm. *Admission:* Free. *Site Info:* Free on-site and street parking. Wheelchair accessible. Tour guide available.

Located across the street from the Bradley House, the Henry and Margaret Hoffman Annex houses some of the Presque Isle County Historical Museum exhibits. These include the John Bunton Collection of more than 1,000 cameras and projectors and other photographic equipment; materials related to the World's Largest Limestone Quarry; and photos, models, and artifacts from the Bradley Transportation Fleet.

Presque Isle County Historical Museum (The Bradley House)

176 W. Michigan Ave., Rogers City, MI 49779 (45.419984, -83.817840)
(989) 734-0123, bradleymuseum@yahoo.com,
www.thebradleyhouse.org
Hours: May-Dec: Wed-Sun 12:30-4:30pm. *Admission:* Free. *Site Info:* Free street parking. Not wheelchair accessible. Tour guide available; large groups should call the museum in advance. Children under 12 must be accompanied by a responsible adult.

Built in 1914, the Bradley House was sold to the Michigan Limestone and Chemical Co. the following year. The "Limestone King" Carl D. Bradley and his family lived there until his death in 1928 and the house was continually occupied by whomever served as the head of the company through 1960. Today, the building is listed in the National Register of Historic Places and houses the Presque Isle County Historical Museum.

ROSCOMMON

Civilian Conservation Corps Museum

11747 N. Higgins Lake Drive, Roscommon, MI 48653 (44.514869, -84.760658)
(989) 348-2537, museuminfo@michigan.gov,
www.michigan.gov/cccmuseum
Hours: May 27-Sep 2: Daily 10am-4pm. *Admission:* Free, although a Michigan State Parks Recreation Passport is required for entry. *Site Info:* Free on-site parking. Wheelchair accessible.

More than 100,000 young men worked in Michigan's forests during the Great Depression and lived in barracks like those on display at the Civilian Conservation Corps Museum. See how "Roosevelt's Tree Army" served the state, creating a legacy still enjoyed today.

Roscommon Area Historical Society

404 Lake St., Roscommon, MI 48653 (44.4956753, -84.5957669)
(989) 344-7386
Hours: Memorial Day to Sep: Fri-Sat 12-4pm. *Admission:* Free. *Site Info:* Free street parking. Wheelchair accessible. Tour guide available by appointment; contact Sharon Boushelle at (989) 275-6131 or Carol Garlo at (989) 275-5835.

The Roscommon Area Historical Society's museum is located in the 1880s-built Gallimore Boarding House that operated from 1904 to 1931. The Richardson School House served the community from 1914 to 1955 and now displays many artifacts depicting the history of the Roscommon and Higgins Lake areas.

THOMPSONVILLE

Michigan Legacy Art Park

12500 Crystal Mountain Drive, Thompsonville, MI 49683
(44.519260, -85.990655)
(231) 378-4963, director@michlegacyartpark.org,
www.michlegacyartpark.org
Hours: Daily during daylight hours. *Admission:* Adults $5, Children free. *Site Info:* Free on-site and street parking. Partially wheelchair accessible; call ahead to reserve a golf cart tour. Self-guided.

The 30-acre Michigan Legacy Art Park boasts a collection of 44 major works of art and 30 poetry stones that help express the Michigan experience. At each sculpture, interpretive signs help visitors to understand the people, events, and natural resources that have shaped the state.

TRAVERSE CITY

History Center of Traverse City

322 Sixth St., Traverse City, MI 49684 (44.761987, -85.627119)
(231) 995-0313, museum@traversehistory.org,
www.traversehistory.org
Hours: Summer: Mon-Sat 10am-5pm, Sun 12-5pm. *Admission:* General public $5, Children (0-4) free. *Site Info:* Free on-site parking. Wheelchair accessible. Self-guided. Visit *www.magical-history-tour.com* for information about the museum's tours of the city.

The History Center of Traverse City includes a pre-written history wing, which features Native American items, a wigwam, and interactive glacier panels depicting the two glaciers that formed Michigan. Children can dig through 2,000 pounds of cherry pits to forge for a souvenir copper ingot, arrow head, Petoskey stone, or beach stone. The Railroad Historical Society of Northwest Michigan also maintains a railroad exhibit at the center.

Maritime Heritage Alliance
13268 S. West Bayshore Drive, Traverse City, MI 49684
(44.786167, -85.638234)
(231) 946-2647, info@maritimeheritagealliance.org,
www.maritimeheritagealliance.org
Hours: Call for hours. *Admission:* Free. *Site Info:* Call ahead for tour guide availability.

The Maritime Heritage Alliance owns a replica of the 1850s schooner *Madeline,* on which the organization offers complimentary sails on certain afternoons and evenings when the ship is in its home port. Visitors can also stop by a replica of the armed sloop *Welcome* when it is in its port. Both boats are official Tall Ships of Michigan. Also available for viewing is also a collection of vintage canoes.

WEST BRANCH

Ogemaw County Historical Museum
123 S. 5th St., West Branch, MI 48661 (44.275833, -84.241029)
(989) 343-0177, oghs1978@gmail.com,
www.westbranch.com/ogemaw_genealogical.htm
Hours: Thu-Fri 10am-2pm. Also by appointment. *Admission:*
Donations accepted. *Site Info:* Street parking. Not wheelchair accessible.

The Ogemaw County Genealogical and Historical Society provides walking tours of the cities and cemeteries as well as driving tours of the county's various historic sites. The museum's exhibits change periodically.

UPPER PENINSULA

BARAGA

Baraga County Historical Museum

803 U.S. Hwy 41, Baraga, MI 49908 (46.771394, -88.491654)
(906) 353-8444, baragacountyhistory@gmail.com,
www.baragacountyhistoricalmuseum.com
Hours: Mon-Thu and Sat 11am-3pm. *Admission:* Adults $2, Youth
$1, Children (0-11) free. *Site Info:* Free on-site parking. Wheelchair
accessible.Tour guide available.

Exhibits at the Baraga County Historical Museum include logging
and lumbering artifacts, the life of Captain James Bendry, the
founding of the Village of Baraga, Bishop Frederic Baraga's
missionary work in Upper Michigan, displays on everyday life in the
late 19th and early 20th centuries, and an exhibit on Finnish
immigrants and their influence on Baraga County. Outdoor exhibits
include a Pettibone Cary-Lift.

BOIS BLANC ISLAND

Bois Blanc Island Historical Society and Museum
1030 W. Huron Drive, Bois Blanc Island, MI 49775 (45.733167, -84.471221)
Hours: Jul to Labor Day: Tue, Thu, and Sat 10am-2pm. *Admission:* Donations accepted. *Site Info:* On-site parking. Partially wheelchair accessible; small step at side entrance. Tour guide available.

The Bois Blanc Island Historical Society and Museum promotes the history of Bois Blanc Island.

BRIMLEY

Wheels of History Museum
Depot Street and M-221, Brimley, MI 49715 (46.406772, -84.572303)
(906) 248-3487, euprussell@yahoo.com, www.baymillsbrimleyhistory.org
Hours: June 20 to Labor Day: Wed-Sun 10am-4pm. *Admission:* Free. *Site Info:* Free street parking. Partially wheelchair accessible. Tour guide available.

Exhibits at the Wheels of History Museum consider the history of the railroad in the Brimley area, the historic Bay Mills townsite, early telephone and communications networks, logging and milling of lumber, Lake Superior fishing and fishing boats, and daily life in early Brimley.

Point Iroquois Light Station
12942 W. Lakeshore Drive, Brimley, MI 49715 (46.484239, -84.632234)
(906) 248-3487, euprussell@yahoo.com, www.baymillsbrimleyhistory.org
Hours: May 15-Oct 15: Daily 9am-5pm. *Admission:* Donations accepted. *Site Info:* Partially wheelchair accessible. Self-guided; tower is open for climbing.

Built in 1855, the Point Iroquois Light Station was last occupied in the 1950s and was placed in the National Register of Historic Places in 1975. It houses a museum featuring a 1950s living room and kitchen, clothing worn by light keepers, complete lists of the names of past lighthouse keepers and caretakers, keepers' logs of weather and ships, and a Fresnel light.

CALUMET

Calumet Visitor Center

98 Fifth St., Calumet, MI 49913 (47.244090, -88.452660)
(906) 337-3168, www.nps.gov/kewe
Hours: Late May to early Sep: Mon-Fri 9am-5pm. Mid-Sep to late
May: Call ahead for hours. *Admission:* Free. *Site Info:* Free on-site
and street parking, Wheelchair accessible. Self-guided.

Operated by Keweenaw National Historical Park, the Calumet
Visitor Center is located in the Union Building, a former lodge hall
for various fraternal organizations. Three floors of interactive
exhibits, films, and museum pieces show what life was like for
residents of the mining community from its establishment through
the closure of the Calumet & Hecla Mining Company in 1968.

Coppertown USA Mining Museum

25815 Red Jacket Road, Calumet, MI 49913 (47.242186,
-88.448189)
(906) 337-4354, www.uppermichigan.com/coppertown
Hours: Jun-Oct: Mon-Sat 11am-5pm. *Admission:* Adults $4,
Children (6-15) $2, Golden Age Pass $3. *Site Info:* Free parking.
Wheelchair accessible. Self-guided.

A Heritage Site of the Keweenaw National Historical Park, the
Coppertown USA Mining Museum features 100 displays in the
former Calumet and Hecla Pattern Shop. These displays introduce
the story of the Copper Country and America's first real mining
boom. A copper knife, for instance, dates back hundreds of years to
the Copper Culture Indians. Other attractions include a 13-minute
video about Keweenaw copper, a simulated mine shaft, railroad
memorabilia, a shoe shop, and old school exhibits.

Norwegian Lutheran Church

338 Seventh St., Calumet, MI 49913 (47.247190, -88.444416)
(906) 337-3731, www.nlc-calumet.org
Hours: Jun-Oct: Daily 9am-5pm. *Admission:* Donations accepted.
Site Info: Free street parking. Not wheelchair accessible. Self-
guided.

Built in 1898, the Norwegian Lutheran Church contains its original
altar, pews, organ, chandelier, and tin ceiling. Storyboards in the
entry share the church's history, a list of its ministers, and photos of
the people who were instrumental in the building and maintaining of
the church and attached parsonage.

CASPIAN

Iron County Historical Museum
100 Brady Ave., Caspian, MI 49915 (46.067802, -88.626229)
(906) 265-2617, info@ironcountyhistoricalmuseum.org,
www.ironcountyhistoricalmuseum.org
Hours: Jun-Sep: Mon-Sat 10am-4pm, Sun 1-4pm. *Admission:*
Adults $8, Seniors $7, Youth (5-18) $3, Children (0-4) free. *Site
Info:* Free on-site parking. Partially wheelchair accessible. Self-
guided.

Located on the former site of the Caspian Mine, the Iron County
Historical Museum has 26 buildings and more than 100 exhibits.
Exhibits reflect the multi-ethnic groups who settled in Iron County
to work in the major industries of iron mining and logging. Other
highlights include the home of Carrie Jacobs-Bond (the composer of
"I Love You Truly" and "Perfect Day") and the Giovanelli Italianate
Gallery, which features Renaissance art.

CEDARVILLE

Les Cheneaux Historical Museum
105 S. Meridian Road, Cedarville, MI 49719 (45.997619,
-84.362911)
(906) 484-2821, lcha@cedarville.net, www.lchistorical.org
Hours: Memorial Day Weekend to Sep: Mon-Sat 10am-5pm.
Admission: Donations accepted. *Site Info:* Free parking. Wheelchair
accessible. Self-guided.

Founded in 1968, Les Cheneaux Historical Museum displays Native
American crafts, logging-era tools, a model of a lumber camp, and
exhibits pertaining to early settlers and hotels/tourism.

Les Cheneaux Maritime Museum
602 E. M-134, Cedarville, MI 49719 (45.999205, -84.350522)
(906) 484-2821, lcha@cedarville.net, www.lchistorical.org
Hours: Memorial Day Weekend to Sep: Mon-Sat 10am-5pm.
Admission: Donations accepted. *Site Info:* Free parking. Partially
wheelchair accessible. Self-guided.

Les Cheneaux Maritime Museum is located in the O.M. Reif
Boathouse (c. 1920). Displays include vintage boats, marine
artifacts, antique outboard motors, and historic photos. The
association also provides boat-building workshops.

CHASSELL

Chassell Heritage Center
42373 Hancock St., Chassell, MI 49916 (47.026802, -88.527195)

(906) 523-1155, www.einerlei.com/community/CHO.html
Hours: Jul-Aug: Tue 1-4pm, Thu 4-9pm. *Admission:* Donations accepted. *Site Info:* Free on-site parking. Not wheelchair accessible. Tour guide available during open hours or by appointment.

A Heritage Site of Keweenaw National Historical Park, the Chassell Heritage Center is located in a former elementary school. Exhibits include local strawberry farming, vintage clothing, a township timeline, three consecutive boys' basketball state championships (1956-58), and the Chassell Lions Club. It is also the home of the Friends of Fashion Vintage Clothing Collection.

COPPER HARBOR

Fort Wilkins Historic Complex
Copper Harbor Lighthouse
15223 U.S. 41, Copper Harbor, MI 49918 (47.466092, -87.877042)
(906) 289-4215, jamesb@michigan.gov,
www.michigan.gov/fortwilkins

Fort Wilkins Historic Complex
Hours: Mid-May to mid-Oct: Daily 8:30am to dusk. *Admission:* Free, although a Michigan State Parks Recreation Passport is required for entry. *Site Info:* Free on-site parking. Wheelchair accessible.

Built in 1844 on the rugged shoreline of Lake Superior, Fort Wilkins is a well-preserved example of mid-19th century army life. It includes 19 buildings—12 of which are original structures dating to the 1840s. There are hands-on exhibits, interpretive signs, and a historical video titled "Beyond the Wilderness: The Fort Wilkins Story."

Copper Harbor Lighthouse
Hours: 10am-6pm. *Admission:* Free, although there is a charge for boat transportation to and from the lighthouse. *Site Info:* Free on-site parking. Wheelchair accessible. Self-guided.

Marking the entrance to one of Michigan's northernmost harbors, the Copper Harbor Lighthouse complex includes the 1844 lighthouse, restored 1848 light keeper's dwelling, and 1933 steel tower.

COVINGTON

Covington Township Historical Museum
East Elm Street and Elm Street, Covington, MI 49919 (46.542070, -88.537348)

(906) 355-2413, marypt@jamadots.com
Hours: Fri-Sat 11am-3pm. *Admission:* Donations accepted. *Site Info:* Free street parking. Self-guided.

Established in 1997, the Covington Historical Society maintains a museum in the former township hall, where exhibits include the area's first fire truck, a horse-drawn cutter, a military display, and a jail cell used to house only one prisoner.

CRYSTAL FALLS

Harbour House Museum
17 N. 4th St., Crystal Falls, MI 49920 (46.096938, -88.332558)
(906) 875-4341, alfred.pieper@gmail.com,
www.harbourhousemuseum.org
Hours: May 30-Aug 31: Thu-Sat 10am-2pm. *Admission:* Individuals $2, Family $5. *Site Info:* Free street parking. Partially wheelchair accessible; first floor only. Tour guide available.

Built in 1900 by master mason and bricklayer Fred Floodstrand, the Harbour House Museum was constructed with cement blocks and designed in the "steamboat" style of architecture with wraparound twin porches. The first floor has been restored to a turn-of-the-century setting, and includes a kitchen, dining room, parlor, and library.

CURTIS

Curtis Historical Society Museum
N9224 Portage Ave., Curtis, MI 49820 (46.206034, -85.747678)
(906) 586-3382, genilady@hughes.net
Hours: Mon-Fri 1-4pm. *Admission:* Donations accepted. *Site Info:* On-site parking. Wheelchair accessible. Self-guided; volunteer available for questions.

The Curtis Historical Society Museum houses artifacts from early logging and settlers. Exhibits include displays about schools, the military, and Native Americans.

DETOUR VILLAGE

DeTour Passage Historical Museum
104 Elizabeth St., DeTour Village, MI 49725 (45.992485, -83.899146)
(906) 297-3231, www.drlps.com
Hours: Daily 1-5pm. *Admission:* Free. *Site Info:* Street parking. Wheelchair accessible.

The DeTour Passage Historical Museum features displays relating to early marine operations, social and governmental activities, pioneer families, Native American history, and life in the early years of the DeTour area.
Information may not be current.

DeTour Reef Light

Located in Lake Huron, three miles south of DeTour Village (45.948922, -83.90305)
(906) 493-6303, drlps@drlps.com, www.drlps.com
Hours: Summer: By appointment. *Site Info:* Free on-site parking. Not wheelchair accessible. Tours are guided and cost $95/person. Children accompanied by parent/guardian receive 50 percent discount.

Built in 1931, the offshore DeTour Reef Light was manned until its automation in 1974. Also on site is a five-foot scale model of the 60-foot DeTour Reef Light crib and an original, working F2T foghorn. Visitors take a 10-minute charter boat ride from Drummond Island to the lighthouse where they climb a 20-foot vertical ladder to the pier deck. Tours last about 2.5 hours.

EAGLE HARBOR

Eagle Harbor Lighthouse Complex

670 Lighthouse Road, Eagle Harbor, MI, 49950 (47.459741, -88.159189)
(906) 289-4990, aboggio@pasty.com, vjamison@pasty.com, www.keweenawhistory.org
Hours: Jul-Aug: Mon-Sat 10am-5pm; Jun and Sep-Oct: Sun 12-5pm. *Admission:* Adults $4.

Originally built in 1851, the Eagle Harbor Lighthouse has aided ships for more than 150 years and is still operational. The lighthouse and its station maintain three additional museums, including a maritime museum, a Keweenaw history museum, and a commercial fishing museum.
Information may not be current.

Rathbone School

200 Center St., Eagle Harbor, MI 49950 (47.457257, -88.162818)
(906) 289-4990, aboggio@pasty.com, vjamison@pasty.com, www.keweenawhistory.org
Hours: Mid-Jun to early Oct. *Admission:* Donations accepted.

Exhibits in the restored 1853 Eagle Harbor School commemorate the birthplace of the Knights of Pythias, a fraternal order founded by Justus H. Rathbone in the 1860s.
Information may not be current.

ENGADINE

Engadine Historical Museum

W14075 Melville St., Engadine, MI 49827 (46.116397, -85.573600)
(906) 477-6908, edchar1@earthlink.net
Hours: Tue and Sat 10am-2pm. *Admission:* Free. *Site Info:* Free
street parking. Wheelchair accessible. Tour guide available.

The Engadine Historical Museum reflects life in the late 1800s and
early 1900s. Displays focus on the lumbering and agricultural eras,
the Cooperidge Mill, old Mackinac County Bank, and more. There
is also a restored log house, built in 1895, on the property.

ESCANABA

Delta County Historical Society & Museum
Sand Point Lighthouse

16 Water Plant Road, Escanaba, MI 49829 (45.744650, -87.043637)
(906) 789-6790, deltacountyhistsoc@sbcglobal.net,
www.deltahistorical.org
Hours: Memorial Day to Labor Day: Daily 11am-4pm. *Admission:*
Adults $3, Children $1, Family $5. *Site Info:* Free parking. Museum
partially wheelchair accessible; lighthouse is not. Self-guided.

The Delta County Historical Society is located in a former radio
station that was recently renovated. While it is located at the same
location, its new address will soon become 16 Beaumier Way,
Escanaba. Exhibits highlight local history including domestic,
commercial, athletic, and military heritage. Also on site is the Sand
Point Lighthouse, which along with its home and boathouse, is open
to visitors.
*Information may not be current.

GARDEN

Fayette Historic Townsite

4785 II Road, Garden, MI 49835 (45.725071, -86.640779)
(906) 644-2603, *www.michigan.gov/fayettetownsite*
Hours: May-Oct. See website or call for hours. *Admission:* Free,
although a Michigan State Park Passport is required for entry. *Site
Info:* On-site parking. Partially wheelchair accessible. Tour guide
available mid-Jun through mid-Aug.

The Fayette Historic Townsite was once an industrial community
that manufactured charcoal pig iron from 1867-1891. Today, it
features a modern visitors center, 19 historic structures, museum
exhibits, and a walking tour, all of which interpret Fayette's role as a
company town.

Garden Peninsula Historical Society Museum

6347 State St., Garden, MI 49835 (45.776855, -86.553120)
Hours: Wed-Sat 11am-3pm. *Admission:* Free. *Site Info:* Free street parking. Wheelchair accessible. Self-guided.

Located in a former schoolhouse, the Garden Peninsula Historical Society Museum highlights local history and includes a genealogy department.

GRAND MARAIS

Lightkeeper's House Museum

E22050 Coast Guard Point Road, Grand Marais, MI 49839
(46.626244, -86.180144)
(906) 494-2404, gmhistoricalsociety@gmail.com,
http://historicalsociety.grandmaraismichigan.com
Hours: Jun and Sep: Sat-Sun 1-4pm; Jul-Aug: Daily 1-4pm.
Admission: Donations accepted. *Site Info:* Free street parking. Not wheelchair accessible. Tour guide available.

Built in 1906, this museum is the restored residence of the Grand Marais lightkeeper and has been furnished in the style of the period.

Old Post Office Museum

N14272 Lake Ave., Grand Marais, MI 49839 (46.671379, -85.984867)
(906) 494-2404, gmhistoricalsociety@gmail.com,
http://historicalsociety.grandmaraismichigan.com
Hours: Jun-Sep: Daily. *Admission:* Donations accepted. *Site Info:* Free street parking. Wheelchair accessible. Self-guided.

The Old Post Office Museum showcases the history of Grand Marais from its early settlement to the present day. A memorial rose garden is located behind the museum.

Pickle Barrel House Museum

N14252 Lake Ave., Grand Marais, MI 49839 (46.670955, -85.984781)
Hours: Jun and Sep: Sat-Sun 1-4pm, Jul-Aug: Daily 1-4pm.
Admission: Donations accepted. *Site Info:* Free street parking. Not wheelchair accessible. Tour guide available.

The Pickle Barrel House was built as a summer residence for author/illustrator William Donahey and his wife, author Mary Dickerson Donahey. The 16-foot-high, barrel-shaped house has been furnished in the style of 1926, when it was built. A number of William Donahey's personal effects are on display, including the drawing chair where he created a number of his "Teenie Weenie" cartoons.

GULLIVER

Gulliver Historical Museum and Seul Choix Point Lighthouse
905 S. Seul Choix Road, Gulliver, MI 49840 (45.921333, -85.912313)
(906) 283-3183, msfischer@hughes.net,
www.greatlakelighthouse.com
Hours: Memorial Day to mid-Oct: Daily 10am-6pm. Off-season hours vary. *Admission:* $4. *Site Info:* Tour guide available for group tours by appointment.

Completed in 1895, the Seul Choix Point Lighthouse is now maintained by the Gulliver Historical Society, which operates its museum in the Fog Signal Building. The Lightkeeper's Living Quarters features rooms as they would have been decorated from 1900 to 1930. On display is the uniform of R. Rosie, the light keeper in 1941, along with his family's original china and stemware.

GWINN

Forsyth Township Historical Society
106 Pine St., Gwinn, MI 49841 (46.2791942, -87.4389156)
(906) 346-5413, rpwills@yahoo.com
Hours: Call for hours. *Admission:* Free. *Site Info:* Street parking. Not wheelchair accessible.

Located above the Forsyth Township Hall, the Forsyth Township Historical Society showcases the history of the K.I. Sawyer Air Force Base as well as the area's small mining and railroad villages from the 1860s. There is a special emphasis on the unique "model town" of Gwinn, which was built in 1908 by William Gwinn Mather, the president of the Cleveland-Cliffs Iron Company, and designed by noted Boston landscape architect Warren H. Manning.

HANCOCK

Finnish American Heritage Center
435 Quincy St., Hancock, MI 49930 (47.1266575, -88.5849602)
(906) 487-7347, archives@finlandia.edu,
www.finlandia.edu/FAHC.html
Hours: Mon-Fri 8am-4:30pm. *Admission:* Donations accepted. *Site Info:* Free on-site and street parking. Wheelchair accessible. Self-guided.

As part of the Finlandia University campus, the Finnish American Heritage Center preserves the rich history and heritage of Finnish

Americans in the Copper Country, Michigan, and North America. In addition to the Finnish American Historical Archives, the building has several display areas that highlight Finnish heritage.

Quincy Mine Association, Inc.

49750 U.S. Hwy 41, Hancock, MI 49930 (47.137232, -88.574581) *(906) 482-3101, glenda@quincymine.com, www.quincymine.com Hours:* May-Jun: Fri-Sun 9:30am-5pm; Mid-June to Oct: Daily 9:30am-5pm. *Admission:* Adults $10-$18, Seniors $10-$15, Youth $5-$8. *Site Info:* On-site parking. Partially wheelchair accessible. Tours are guided.

In 1961, the Quincy Mine Hoist Association preserves the mining structures and technology of the Quincy Mine. Today, visitors can tour the association's museum, located in the renovated 1894 Hoist House. They can also explore a section of the mine's seventh level to see what life was like for the mineworkers and learn about changes in mining processes through history.

HERMANSVILLE

IXL Historical Museum

W5561 River St., Hermansville, MI 49847 (45.709251, -87.607201) *(906) 498-2181, museum@hermansville.com, www.hermansville.com/IXLMuseum Hours:* Memorial Day to Labor Day: 12:30-4pm (CDT). *Admission:* Adults $4, Children (0-18) free. *Site Info:* Free on-site parking. Only outer buildings are wheelchair accessible. Tour guide available.

The IXL Historical Museum consists of the original 1881-1882 Office Building of the Wisconsin Land and Lumber Company and IXL Flooring Company of Hermansville. The main building contains lumber and hardwood flooring artifacts as well as the estate furnishings of the Meyer and Earle families. Established during the late 1800s, the main building was in use as an office until 1978 and is listed in the National Register of Historic Places. Surrounding the main office building are a complex of outer buildings, including the original Hermansville Produce Warehouse, IXL Carriage House, a company house, and a train depot.

HOUGHTON

Carnegie Museum of the Keweenaw

105 Huron St., Houghton, MI 49931 (47.1213868, -88.567905) *(906) 482-7140, history@cityofhoughton.com, Find on Facebook Hours:* Oct 1-Jul 3: Tue and Thu 12-5pm, Sat 12-4pm; Jul 5-Sep 30: Tue-Wed 12-5pm, Thu 12-6pm, Fri-Sat 12-4pm. Also by appointment. *Admission:* Free. *Site Info:* Free on-site and street parking. Self-guided.

Built in 1910, Houghton's Carnegie Library now serves as the Carnegie Museum of the Keweenaw. Exhibits are displayed on the main floor.

IRON MOUNTAIN

Cornish Pump Museum
300 Kent Road, Iron Mountain, MI 49801 (45.825177, -88.069906)
(906) 774-4276, mrh-museum@sbcglobal.net,
www.menomineerangehistoricalfoundation.org
Hours: Memorial Day to Labor Day: Tue-Fri 11am-3pm. *Site Info:*
Wheelchair accessible.

The Cornish Pump Museum is home to the largest steam-driven pumping engine ever built in the United States. It also exhibits a rare collection of underground mining equipment used in area iron ore mines.

Menominee Range Historical Museum
300 E. Ludington St., Iron Mountain, MI 49801 (45.820399, -88.063525)
(906) 774-4276, mrh-museum@sbcglobal.net,
www.menomineerangehistoricalfoundation.org
Hours: Memorial Day to Labor Day: Tue-Fri 11am-3pm.
Admission: Adults $5, Seniors $4.50, Students $3, Children (0-9) free. *Site Info:* Not wheelchair accessible. Tour guide available.

The Menominee Range Historical Foundation & Museum preserves the history of Dickinson County. It features more than 100 exhibits depicting life on the Menominee Iron Range from the latter part of the 19th century through the early years of the 20th century.

World War II Glider and Military Museum
302 Kent St., Iron Mountain, MI 49801 (45.825177, -88.069906)
(906) 774-4276, mrh-museum@sbcglobal.net,
www.menomineerangehistoricalfoundation.org
Hours: Mon-Sat 9am-5pm, Sun 12pm-4pm. *Admission:* Students $4, Seniors $7, Adults $8. *Site Info:* Wheelchair accessible.

The World War II Glider and Military Museum contains a completely restored CG-4A WWII glider, a WWII jeep, Ford memorabilia, and military exhibits (Civil War through the Iraq-Afghanistan conflicts).

IRONWOOD

Ironwood Area Historical Society
150 N. Lowell, Ironwood, MI 49938 (46.455196, -90.170722)

(906) 932-0287, twolees1@chartermi.net, www.ironwoodmi.org
Hours: Memorial Day to Labor Day: Mon-Sat 12-4pm. *Admission:*
Free. *Site Info:* On-site parking. Wheelchair accessible. Tour guide
available.

The Ironwood Area Historical Society shares an 1892 depot with the
Ironwood Chamber of Commerce. Exhibits focus on the history of
Gogebic Range and Ironwood and the significance of mining to the
area. There is also a representation of an early general store that is
stocked as it would have been during Ironwood's early days.
Information may not be current.

ISHPEMING

Cliffs Shaft Mining Museum
501 W. Euclid St., Ishpeming, MI 49849 (46.491176, -87.675695)
(906) 485-1882, steelworkers1@aol.com, Find on Facebook
Hours: Tue-Sat 10am-4pm. *Admission:* Adults (18+) $9, Youth (13-
17) $3, Children (0-12) free. *Site Info:* On-site parking. Wheelchair
accessible except for service tunnel tour. Tour guide available.

The Cliffs Shaft Mining Museum provides visitors with a preserved
and complete example of underground iron mining in Michigan.
Information may not be current.

Ishpeming Area Historical Society Museum
501 W. Euclid St., Ishpeming, MI 49849 (46.491752, -87.675002)
ishphistoricalsociety@gmail.com, Find on Facebook.com
Hours: Jun-Sep: Tue-Sat 10am-4pm. *Admission:* Donations
accepted. *Site Info:* Free on-site parking. Wheelchair accessible.
Self-guided.

The Ishpeming Area Historical Society focuses on the everyday life
of Ishpeming's citizens, students, merchants, clubs, organizations,
and past times. It is located in the Cliff's Mine Shaft facility, of
which it is a separate entity.

U.S. Ski & Snowboard Hall of Fame
610 Palms Ave., Ishpeming, MI 49849 (46.503491, -87.665785)
(906) 485-6323, administrator@skihall.com, www.skihall.com
Hours: Mon-Sat 10am-5pm. *Admission:* Donations accepted. *Site
Info:* Free on-site parking. Wheelchair accessible. Tour guide
available.

The U.S. Ski and Snowboard Hall of Fame provides recognition for
those who have achieved national and international success in skiing
and snowboarding competition or who have contributed
significantly to the development of ski sports in the United States.
The museum features 15,000 square feet of exhibits, including the

National Honors Court, Birkebeiner diorama, early American ski manufacturing, the first chair lift in America, 10th Mountain Division Tribute, and more.

KINROSS

Kinross Heritage Park
6277 W. M-80, Kinross, MI 49752 (46.265626, -84.495941)
(906) 440-3840, ksupervisor@kinross.net,
www.kinross.net/heritage.htm
Hours: Thu-Sun 1-5:30pm. *Admission:* Free. *Site Info:* Free parking; call ahead for buses or trailers. Museum and log cabin are wheelchair accessible. Tour guide available.

Seeking to preserve the history of Kinross for future generations, the Kinross Heritage Park includes an 1882 log cabin, a 1902 one-room schoolhouse, a working blacksmith shop, and early farming, household goods, and military displays.
Information may not be current.

LAKE LINDEN

Houghton County Historical Museum
53150 M-26, Lake Linden, MI 49945 (47.187007,-88.412782)
(906) 296-4121, info@houghtonhistory.org,
www.houghtonhistory.org
Hours: Hours vary by season. Call ahead. *Admission:* Adults $5, Seniors $3, Students (6-16) $3. *Site Info:* Free parking. Partially wheelchair accessible. Tour guide available by appointment. Trains run on weekends; tickets are $4/adult, $3/senior, $3/student, and $1/child (0-5).

Exhibits at the Houghton County Historical Museum include Lake Linden & Torch Lake Railroad, a restored 0-4-0 Porter Steam Locomotive, and a 3' gauge track to support tours interpreting the former Calumet & Hecla Mill. The site also houses a general history museum, a 1940s WPA-constructed log cabin, a schoolhouse, and the former First Congregational Church of Lake Linden.

L'ANSE

Ford Center and Historic Ford Sawmill Museum
21235 Alberta Ave. (US-41), L'Anse, MI 49946 (46.643985, -88.480968)
(906) 524-6181, fordcenter@mtu.edu, www.fordcenter.mtu.edu
Hours: Mon-Thu 10am-5pm. *Admission:* Adults $5, Seniors (60+) $3, Children (5-12) $2. *Site Info:* Free on-site parking. Partially wheelchair accessible. Tour guide available by appointment.

Created by Henry Ford in 1935, the Historic Ford Sawmill Museum is owned and operated by Michigan Technological University. Exhibits cover the sawmill's operations, Henry Ford's lumber empire and why he needed so much wood, the history of Alberta, sustainable forestry, and the importance of wood in modern life. Also on site is the Village of Alberta, Ford's concept of a model sawmill town and self-sufficient rural community.

MACKINAC ISLAND

Fort Mackinac
Located on Mackinac Island (45.852222, -84.617222)
(231) 436-4100, mackinacparks@michigan.gov,
www.mackinacparks.com
Hours: Early May to mid-Oct: 9:30am-5pm; hours extended to 6pm during peak summer season. *Admission:* Adults $11, Youth (5-17) $6.50. Fort Mackinac ticket allows entrance to downtown historic buildings during main season. *Site Info:* Partially wheelchair accessible (see "Guide to Access" brochure available at site). Costumed interpretive guides daily.

Fort Mackinac includes 14 original buildings, including one of Michigan's oldest buildings: the Officers' Stone Quarters, which dates back to 1780.

Richard and Jane Manoogian Mackinac Art Museum
7070 Main St., Mackinac Island, MI 49757 (45.848171, -84.618663)
(231) 436-4100, mackinacparks@michigan.gov,
www.mackinacparks.com
Hours: Early May to mid-Oct: 10am-4:30pm; hours extended to 6pm during peak summer season. *Admission:* Adults $5, Youth (5-17) $3.50.

The Richard and Jane Manoogian Mackinac Art Museum showcases the historic artwork in Mackinac State Historic Parks' collection.

MANISTIQUE

Pioneer Park
Deer Street (Northwest of the Indian River Bridge), Manistique, MI 49854 (45.962941, -86.250894)
(906) 341-5045, m085@centurytel.net,
www.cityofmanistique.org/schs
Hours: June to Labor Day: Wed-Sat 1-4pm. *Admission:* $1 donation. *Site Info:* On-site parking. Partially wheelchair accessible. Tour guide available.

The Schoolcraft County Historical Society's museum is located in Manistique's Pioneer Park. This includes the 1923 water tower,

1895 log cabin, and a fire engine building that contains a 19th-century hook-and-ladder truck and 1950 LaFrance fire truck.

MARQUETTE

Beaumier U.P. Heritage Center
1401 Presque Isle Ave., Northern Michigan University, Marquette, MI 49855 (46.558270, -87.402738)
(906) 227-3212, heritage@nmu.edu, www.nmu.edu/beaumier
Hours: 10am-4pm. *Admission:* Free. *Site Info:* Free on-site parking. Wheelchair accessible. Self-guided.

Located in Cohodas Hall, the Beaumier U.P. Heritage Center creates displays related to the history of Northern Michigan University and the Upper Peninsula. The center features two to three temporary exhibitions each year and has a permanent installation on immigration to the Upper Peninsula.

Marquette Regional History Center
145 W. Spring St., Marquette, MI 49855 (46.541410, -87.395704)
(906) 226-3571, mrhc@marquettehistory.org,
www.marquettecohistory.org
Hours: Mon-Tue 10am-5pm, Wed 10am-8pm, Thu-Fri 10am-5pm, Sat 10am-3pm. *Admission:* Adults $7, Seniors $6, Students $3, Children (0-12) $2. *Site Info:* Free on-site parking. Wheelchair accessible. Tour guide available upon request.

The Marquette Regional History Center includes a 7,500-square-foot exhibit space with displays that depict natural history, indigenous peoples, fur trade, pioneer life, sports history, and Yooper life. The organization was the recipient of the Historical Society of Michigan's Superior Award in 01 .

MENOMINEE

Chappee-Webber Learning Center
N1936 River Road, Menominee, MI 49858 (45.1348373, -87.6659068)
(906) 863-9000, jcallow1@new.rr.com, krahgp@new.rr.com,
dmurwin@new.rr.com, www.menomineehistoricalsociety.org
Hours: By appointment. *Admission:* Free. *Site Info:* Free on-site parking. Partially wheelchair accessible. Self-guided.

In the fall, the Chappee-Webber Learning Center brings in special speakers to teach youth about fur trading, horticulture, logging, and Native American life. The site also features a pavilion, historical markers, and the opportunity to walk trails and along the Menominee River.

Heritage Museum

904 11th Ave., Menominee, MI 49858 (45.108708, -87.613386)
(906) 863-9000, jcallow1@new.rr.com, krahgp@new.rr.com,
dmurwin@new.rr.com, www.menomineehistoricalsociety.org
Hours: Memorial Day to Labor Day: Mon-Sat 10am-4pm.
Admission: Donations accepted. *Site Info:* Free on-site and street
parking. Partially wheelchair accessible. Tour guide available;
donations accepted. Large groups should make reservations.

Located in a former church, the Menominee County Historical
Society's Heritage Museum focuses on the area's early history.
Artifacts relate to Native Americans, early settlers, logging, fishing,
trapping, and the development of industry in the county from 1863.

West Shore Fishing Museum

N5156 M-35, Menominee, MI 49887 (45.414034, -87.822126)
(906) 863-9716
Hours: Memorial Day to Labor Day: Sat-Sun 1-4pm. *Admission:*
Donations accepted. *Site Info:* Free on-site parking. Wheelchair
accessible. Tour guide available; group tours by appointment.

The Bailey Property Preservation Association preserves and portrays
the history of the Great Lakes commercial fishing industry, in
particular the history of commercial fishing along the west shore of
Green Bay. Located in Bailey Park, the West Shore Fishing
Museum was once the site of the Charles L. Bailey commercial
fishery. The museum features a restored Victorian family home and
gardens, exhibit building, twine shed, and boat shelter with a fleet of
five commercial fishing boats.

MICHIGAMME

Michigamme Museum

110 Main St., Michigamme, MI 49861 (46.535432, -88.108302)
(906) 323-9016, michigammetownship@gmail.com
Hours: Memorial Day to Sep: 12-5pm. *Admission:* Donations
accepted. *Site Info:* Street parking. Wheelchair accessible. Tour
guide available.

Exhibits at the Michigamme Museum include logging, mining,
"Anatomy of a Murder," a log house, and a 1900 American
LaFrance steam fire engine.

MOHAWK

Central Mine Village

6-10 Central Road, Mohawk, MI 49950 (47.405771, -88.200421)
(906) 289-4990, aboggio@pasty.com, vjamison@pasty.com,
www.keweenawhistory.org

Hours: Year-round, although the visitors center is open only in the summer. *Admission:* Donations accepted.

Once home to more than 1,200 people, the Central Mine is a former company town that the Keweenaw County Historical Society acquired in 1996. The society asks that visitors respect the privacy of dwelling occupants when touring the mine site.
*Information may not be current.

Eagle Harbor Life Saving Station Museum
End of Marina Road, Mohawk, MI 49950 (47.459051, -88.148851)
(906) 289-4990, aboggio@pasty.com, vjamison@pasty.com,
www.keweenawhistory.org
Hours: Mid-Jun to early Oct: Daily 9am-6pm. *Admission:*
Donations accepted.

In honor of those who served in the Life Saving Service (which became part of the U.S. Coast Guard), the Eagle Harbor Life Saving Station Museum features equipment, including surf and lifeboats, used in rescue operations. A special exhibit is dedicated to the station's most famous rescue, the 191 wreck of the steamer *L.C. Waldo.*
*Information may not be current.

Eagle River Museum
MI-26 and 4th Street, Mohawk, MI 49950 (47.412815, -88.296051)
(906) 289-4990, aboggio@pasty.com, vjamison@pasty.com,
www.keweenawhistory.org
Hours: Open mid-Jun-early Oct. *Admission:* Donations accepted.

The Eagle River Museum focuses on the Cliff Mine, the town of Eagle River, the neighboring town and mine of Phoenix, and the amusement area known as Crestview. The museum features objects and exhibits about the Eagle River area.
*Information may not be current.

MUNISING

Alger County Historical Society Heritage Center
1496 Washington St., Munising, MI 49862 (46.424778, -86.625177)
(906) 387-4308, algerchs@jamadots.com
Hours: Thu 5-8pm, Fri 2:30-9pm, Sat 9am-5pm. *Admission:*
Donations accepted. *Site Info:* On-site parking. Wheelchair accessible.

Located in the former Washington Grade School, the Alger County Historical Society Heritage Center highlights the history of Grand Island and the Grand Island Recreation Area, Munising Woodenware Company, barn building, homemaking, Native

Americans, and saunas. There is also a fur trader's cabin and blacksmith shop on site.

NAUBINWAY

Top of the Lake Snowmobile Museum

W11660 Lake Michigan Scenic Hwy (US-2), Naubinway, MI 49762 (46.0944167, -85.450211)
(906) 477-6298, info@snowmobilemuseum.com,
www.snowmobilemuseum.com
Hours: Wed-Mon 11am-5pm. *Admission:* Adults $5, Youth (0-16) free. *Site Info:* On-site parking. Wheelchair accessible. Tour guide available; call ahead for group tours.

Exhibits at the Top of the Lake Snowmobile Museum show how the history of snowmobiling has progressed to the racing era. On display are more than 100 vintage and antique snowmobiles, a wide variety of accessories (suits, helmets, sleighs, classic oil cans, vintage signs, and banners), and a two-man chainsaw with a curious connection to snowmobiles.

NEGAUNEE

Michigan Iron Industry Museum

73 Forge Road, Negaunee, MI 49866 (46.521732, -87.564623)
(906) 475-7857, jamesb@michigan.gov,
www.michigan.gov/ironindustrymuseum
Hours: May-Oct: Daily 9:30am-4:30pm; Nov-Apr: Mon-Fri 9:30am-4pm. *Admission:* Donations accepted. Admission to view film is $1/person; children (0-5) free. *Site Info:* Free on-site parking. Wheelchair accessible. Self-guided.

The Iron Industry Museum overlooks the historic site of the Carp River Forge, the first iron forge in the Lake Superior region. It interprets Michigan's rich iron mining heritage through exhibits, audiovisual programs, and outdoor interpretive trails. The 23-minute documentary "Iron Spirits: Life on the Michigan Iron Range" is shown seven times daily.

NEWBERRY

Crisp Point Lighthouse

1944 Crisp Point Road (CR-412), Newberry, MI 49868 (46.709437, -85.368849)
(517) 230-6294, cplhs@sbcglobal.net,
www.crisppointlighthouse.org
Hours: May-Oct: 10am-5pm. *Admission:* Free. *Site Info:* Free on-site parking. Grounds, visitors center, and restrooms wheelchair accessible; lighthouse is not wheelchair accessible. Self-guided.

The Crisp Point Light Historical Society restores and preserves the Crisp Point Lighthouse for future generations. Attractions at the lighthouse include a Fourth Order Fresnel lens, Fresnel buoy lens, historical photos, artifacts found on the grounds, and various styles of USCG Great Lakes buoys.

Luce County Historical Museum

411 W. Harrie St., Newberry, MI 49868 (46.352712, -85.514174)
(906) 293-3786,
www.exploringthenorth.com/newberry/histmuseum.html
Hours: June to Labor Day: Wed-Fri 1-4pm. Also by appointment.
Admission: Donations accepted. *Site Info:* Free parking. Wheelchair accessible. Tour guide available.

The Luce County Historical Museum is located in the former Sheriff's Residence and Jail, which was built in 1894. The brownstone, Queen Anne-style residence features the original kitchen, dining room, parlor, and bedrooms with related artifacts. Public areas contain the men's and women's jail cells, the sheriff's office, and an 1890 judge's bench with witness stand and jury chairs.

Tahquamenon Logging Museum

North M-123 (South of Tahquamenon River), Newberry, MI 49868 (46.370784, -85.510416)
(906) 293-3700, www.newberrychamber.net
Hours: Daily 10am-5pm. *Admission:* Adults $5, Youth (6-12) $2, Children (0-5) free. *Site Info:* Free on-site parking. Wheelchair accessible. Tour guide available.

The Tahquamenon Logging Museum provides information and artifacts depicting the early logging days. Attractions include an authentic log cook shack, the original Camp Germfask CCC building, bronze CCC statue, Port Huron steam engine #6854, original Williams Family log home, original one-room Pratt school house, and Goldthorpe logging truck.

ONTONAGON

Ontonagon Historical Museum

422 River St., Ontonagon, MI 49953 (46.872107, -89.316975)
(906) 884-6165, ochs@jamadots.com, www.ontonagonmuseum.org
Hours: Tue-Sat 10am-4pm. *Admission:* $3. *Site Info:* Free on-site and street parking. Wheelchair accessible. Self-guided.

The Ontonagon Historical Museum displays collections of mining, logging, farming, marine, and social memorabilia.

Ontonagon Lighthouse

Ontonagon Street (Between factory and river), Ontonagon MI 49953
(46.872679, -89.324885)
(906) 884-6165, ochs@jamadots.com, www.ontonagonmuseum.org
Site Info: Tours are held Tue-Sat at 11am, 1:30pm, and 3:30pm.
Tours begin at the Ontonagon Historical Museum.

Listed in the National Register of Historic Places since 1975, the
Ontonagon Lighthouse includes historical maritime displays.

PAINESDALE

Painesdale Mine Shaft, Inc.

42631 Shafthouse Road, Painesdale, MI 49955 (47.040368,
-88.668910)
*(906) 231-5542, painesdalemineshaft@yahoo.com,
www.painesdalemineshaft.com*
Hours: By appointment. *Admission:* Free. *Site Info:* Free street
parking. Partially wheelchair accessible (Shafthouse and Hoist
Buildings). Self-guided.

Painesdale Mine Shaft, Inc. seeks to preserve and interpret the
Champion #4 Copper Mine Shafthouse, which was built in 1902 and
operated until 1967. The organization offers tours of the shafthouse,
hoist house, and mining captain's office.

PARADISE

Great Lakes Shipwreck Museum

18335 N. Whitefish Point Road, Paradise, MI 49768 (46.771019,
-84.957811)
*(906) 635-1742, blynn@shipwreckmuseum.com,
www.shipwreckmuseum.com*
Hours: May-Oct: Daily 10am-6pm. *Admission:* Adults $13, Youth
$9, Children (0-5) free, Family $35. *Site Info:* Free parking.
Wheelchair accessible. Self-guided. For group tours of 20 or more,
call ahead.

Located at Whitefish Point, the site of oldest active lighthouse on
Lake Superior, the Great Lakes Shipwreck Museum includes
artifacts and exhibits concerning the sailors and ships who braved
the waters of Superior. On display is the bell of *Edmund Fitzgerald,*
the restored 1849 Light Keepers' Quarters, and more. The lighthouse
tower is closed to the public.
Information may not be current.

PICKFORD

Pickford Museum

175 E. Main St., Pickford, MI 49774 (46.157995, -84.360738)
(906) 647-1372, kdschmitigal@centurylink.net,
www.pickfordmuseum.org
Hours: Memorial Day to Labor Day: Mon-Sat 10am-3pm; Labor
Day to Oct: Fri-Sat 10am-3pm. *Admission:* Donations accepted. *Site
Info:* Free street parking. Self-guided. Private tours by appointment;
call Dianne at (906) 297-3013 or Carol at (906) 647-8533.

The Pickford Museum is located in a restored car dealership and
hardware building that was originally built in 1912. Today, the
building is listed in the National Register of Historic Places and
showcases life in the area from 1877 to the present. A section of the
museum is devoted to ancestral portraits and a large collection of
family genealogies.

PHOENIX

Bammert Blacksmith Shop

MI-26 (North of US-41), Phoenix, MI 49950 (47.392635,
-88.276551)
(906) 289-4990, aboggio@pasty.com, vjamison@pasty.com,
www.keweenawhistory.org
Hours: Mid-May to early Oct. *Admission:* Donations accepted.

Built in the 1880s at the Cliff Mine location, the Bammert
Blacksmith Shop was moved to Phoenix around 1906. It is named
for Amos Bammert, who operated the shop until his death in 1940.
Today, the shop displays many items used by the blacksmith and by
people who pioneered the Keweenaw.
*Information may not be current.

Phoenix Church of the Assumption

Corner of MI-26 and US-41, Phoenix, MI 49950 (47.389092,
-88.276431)
(906) 289-4990, aboggio@pasty.com, vjamison@pasty.com,
www.keweenawhistory.org
Hours: Open mid-Jun to early Oct. *Admission:* Donations accepted.

Originally built in 1858 at the Clifton townsite, the Church of the
Assumption was moved to Phoenix in 1899. Today, the church is
deconsecrated, but is still used for weddings and other services. As a
museum, it contains artifacts from every Catholic Church in
Houghton and Keweenaw Counties, past and present.
*Information may not be current.

REPUBLIC

Pascoe House Museum

183 Cedar St., South Republic, MI 49879 (46.364017, -87.980917)
(906) 376-2258, lavantl@aol.com,
www.republicmichigan.com/history.php
Hours: Memorial Day to Labor Day: Sat-Sun 1-3pm. Also by
appointment. *Admission:* Donations accepted. *Site Info:* Free street
parking. Partially wheelchair accessible; downstairs only. Tour
guide available by appointment; call (906) 376-2258 or (906) 376-
2332.

Operated by the Republic Area Historical Society, the Pascoe House
is an unaltered 1880s house built by the early mining company. The
museum features an illustrated timeline of Republic, Witch Lake,
and Black River history; recreated rooms from 1900; and more. The
society also maintains interpretive signs—concerning mining and
town history—south of Munson Park.

ROCKLAND

Rockland Township Historical Museum

40 National Ave., Rockland, MI 49960 (46.733081, -89.179158)
(906) 886-2821
Hours: Memorial Day to Sep: Daily 11:30am-4:30pm. Also by
appointment. *Admission:* Free. *Site Info:* Wheelchair accessible.

The Rockland Township Historical Museum is dedicated to the
history of Rockland Township's people, copper mines, businesses,
and Michigan's first telephone system. Home settings include
kitchen, dining room, parlor, and bedroom. There are also mining,
farming, school, and military displays.

SAULT STE. MARIE

Baaweting Anishinaabe Interpretive Center

523 Ashmun St., Sault Ste. Marie, MI 49783 (46.497033,
-84.348344)
(906) 635-6050, www.saultstemarie.com
Hours: Call ahead.

A community-driven effort of the Sault Ste. Marie Tribe of
Chippewa Indians, the Baaweting Anishinaabe Interpretive Center
educates people about the Native American point of view and the
"Anishinaabe Bimaadiziwin," or native life ways.
*Information may not be current.

Chippewa County Historical Society

115 Ashmun St., Sault Ste. Marie, MI 49783 (46.501060, -84.345606)

(906) 635-7082, cchs@sault.com, www.cchsmi.com
Hours: Apr-Dec: Mon-Fri 1-4pm. *Admission:* Donations accepted.
Site Info: On-site and street parking. Wheelchair access at back entrance; call ahead.

The Chippewa County Historical Society is located in the 1889 building that originally housed the *Sault Ste. Marie News*, which was owned by Chase S. Osborn, Michigan's only governor to come from the Upper Peninsula. Displays relate to the railroad, Chase Osborn, Native Americans, and the telephone.

Museum Ship *Valley Camp*

501 E. Water St., Sault Ste. Marie, MI 49783 (46.498648, -84.337391)

(906) 632-3658, admin@saulthistoricsites.com, www.saulthistoricsites.com
Hours: Mid-May to mid-Oct. Call or see website for hours.
Admission: Combination tickets and group rates available. *Site Info:* Free on-site parking. Partially wheelchair accessible. Tour guide available.

This 550-foot bulk carrier was built in 1917, sailed until 1966, and was converted into a maritime museum in 1968. Visitors view all parts of the *Valley Camp* to see how a 29-person crew lived and worked. The cargo hold has displays of artifacts, paintings, shipwreck items, models, and exhibits related to maritime history.

River of History Museum

531 Ashmun St., Sault Ste. Marie, MI 49783 (46.4968357, -84.3482555)

(906) 632-1999, admin@saulthistoricsites.com, www.riverofhistory.org
Hours: Mid-May to mid-Oct: Mon-Sat 11am-5pm. Closed major holidays. *Admission:* Adults $7, Children $3.50. *Site Info:* Wheelchair accessible. Free audio wands available.

The River of History Museum tells the 8,000-year history of the St. Marys River Valley, from its glacial origins to Native American occupation, French fur trade, British expansion, and U.S. independence.

Tower of History

326 E. Portage St., Sault Ste. Marie, MI 49783 (46.498141, -84.340538)

(906) 632-3658, admin@saulthistoricsites.com, www.saulthistoricsites.com

Hours: Mid-May to mid-Oct: Daily 10am-5pm. *Admission:*
Combination tickets and group rates available. *Site Info:* On-site and
street parking. Not wheelchair accessible.

The 210-foot Tower of History shares local and Native American
history, the story of the early missionaries, and other exhibits. The
upper level features a 360-degree view of the Sault Locks and
surrounding area.

Water Street Historic Block
405 E. Water St., Sault Ste. Marie, MI 49783 (46.498778,
-84.337757)
*(906) 632-3658, admin@saulthistoricsites.com,
www.saulthistoricsites.com*
Admission: Donations accepted. *Site Info:* Street parking.
Wheelchair accessible. Tour guide available.

This cooperative effort between the Chippewa County Historical
Society, Sault Historic Sites, and the City of Sault Ste. Marie
includes the 1793 home of early fur trader John Johnston, the Henry
Rowe Schoolcraft Office (Schoolcraft was the first Indian Agent in
the United States), and the Kemp Industrial Museum (a museum of
local industries in the former Kemp Coal Company office).

SOUTH RANGE

Copper Range Historical Museum
44 Trimountain Ave., South Range, MI 49963 (47.0698088,
-88.643583)
*(906) 482-6125, johnandjeanp@chartermi.net,
www.pasty.com/crhm*
Hours: Jun: Tue-Fri 12-3pm; Jul-Aug: Mon-Fri 12-3pm; Sep: Tue-
Fri 12-3pm. Also by appointment; call (906) 482-3097 or (906) 487-
9412. *Admission:* $1 donation. *Site Info:* Free street parking.
Partially wheelchair accessible. Tour guide available; group tours
available by appointment.

The Copper Range Historical Museum creates a sense of what the
life and work experience was like during the copper mining era. The
museum features samples of pure copper, a "cooper" and his tools
for making barrels, stereoscope and accompanying photos, photos of
area mining-related sites, and mining memorabilia. Other items on
display include photos of local music hall-of-fame winners, artifacts
from the Copper Range Railroad and Bus Line, former Busch
Brewery and South Range Baseball team memorabilia, and more.

ST. HELENA ISLAND

St. Helena Island Light Station
Southeast Corner of St. Helena Island (45.854913, -84.863634)
(231) 436-5580, info@gllka.com, www.gllka.com
Hours: Visitors with own boat can visit anytime. *Admission:*
Donations accepted. *Site Info:* Boat access only. Not wheelchair
accessible. Tour guide available mid-Jun to mid-Aug.

The Great Lakes Lighthouse Keepers Association is a steward of the
St. Helena Island Light Station, a fully restored light station with
live-in volunteer keeper program.

ST. IGNACE

Father Marquette National Memorial Museum
720 Church St., St. Ignace, MI 49781 (45.853417, -84.727697)
(906) 643-8620, burnettw@michigan.gov,
www.michigan.gov/marquettememorial
Hours: Daily 8am-10pm. *Admission:* Free, although a Michigan
State Recreation Passport is required for entry to the park. *Site Info:*
Public parking. Wheelchair accessible. Self-guided.

The Father Marquette National Memorial Museum is dedicated to
the memory of missionary and explorer Father Jacques Marquette.
The museum recommends taking about one hour to tour the
memorial, 15-station outdoor interpretive trail, and panoramic views
of the Mackinac Bridge.

Fort de Buade Museum
334 N. State St., St. Ignace, MI 49781 (45.868646, -84.727886)
(906) 643-6627, fortdebuademuseum@gmail.com,
www.michilimackinachistoricalsociety.com
Hours: Tue-Thu 10am-6pm, Fri 10am-9pm, Sat 10am-6pm.
Admission: Donations accepted. *Site Info:* Metered street parking.
Partially wheelchair accessible. Tour guide available by
appointment for a fee.

On display at the Fort de Buade Museum are the Newberry Tablets,
thought to be relics of the copper culture that traded with
Mediterranean civilizations in 1000 B.C. Other exhibits include
Native American collection artifacts, a representation of Chief
Satigo's lodge, and a display relating to early St. Ignace and
Northern Michigan.

Museum of Ojibwa Culture
500 N. State St., St. Ignace, MI 49781 (45.871551, -84.731304)
(906) 643-9161, ojibmus@lighthouse.net,
www.museumofojibwaculture.net

Hours: Memorial Day Weekend to mid-October: Daily. *Admission:* Donations accepted.

Experience how Ojibwa and Huron Indians and the French lived in the Straits area 300 years ago. The museum shares the culture of the Ojibwa people and explores how the French Jesuit missionary Jacques Marquette influenced the Indians' lives.
Information may not be current.

VULCAN

Iron Mountain Iron Mine

US-2 and Belrose Street, Vulcan, MI 49892 (45.782489, -87.864789)
(906) 563-8077, ironmine@uplogon.com,
www.ironmountainironmine.com
Hours: Memorial Day to Oct 15: Daily 9am-5pm CDT. *Admission:* Adults $12, Children (6-12) $7.50, Children (0-5) free. *Site Info:* On-site parking. Wheelchair accessible. Guided tours included in admission.

Located nine miles east of Iron Mountain, the Iron Mountain Iron Mine keeps alive the heritage of the area's underground mining ancestors. The site provides guided underground mine tours of the former east Vulcan mine, which produced more than 22 million tons of iron ore from 1870-1945.

WAKEFIELD

Wakefield Museum

306 Sunday Lake Street, Wakefield, MI 49968 (46.474923, -89.941495)
(906) 224-1045, djferson@att.net
Hours: Jun-Sep: Tue-Sat 1-4pm. *Admission:* Donations accepted.
Site Info: Street parking available in front of museum. Not wheelchair accessible. Tour guide available.

Operated by the Wakefield Historical Society, the Wakefield Museum features a period classroom, doctor's office, kitchen, and general store. There is also a veterans' display, mining exhibit, and "Esther's Closet," which features period fashions.

INDEX

Fighting Falcon Military Museum, Greenville, 50
Finnish American Heritage Center, Hancock, 148
Fire Barn Museum: Muskegon, 27
Flat Rock, 84
Flint, 84
Florence B. Dearing Museum, Hartland, 90
Flushing, 86
Flushing Area Museum and Cultural Center, Flushing, 86
Ford Center and Historic Ford Sawmill Museum, L'Anse, 152
Ford Piquette Avenue Plant, Detroit, 79
Ford Rouge Factory Tour, Dearborn, 78
Ford-MacNichol Home, Wyandotte, 116
Forsyth Township Historical Society, Gwinn, 148
Fort de Buade Museum,: St. Ignace, 164
Fort Gratiot Light Station, Port Huron, 102
Fort Mackinac, Mackinac Island, 153
Fort Wilkins Historic Complex, Copper Harbor, 143
Fowlerville, 47
Frankenmuth, 48
Frankenmuth Historical Association Museum, Frankenmuth, 48
Frankfort, 123
Fraser, 86
Friend Hack House Museum, Milan, 94
G.A.R. Hall, Marshall, 55
Gagetown, 86
Galesburg, 17
Galesburg Historical Museum, Galesburg, 17
Garden, 146
Garden City, 87
Garden City Historical Museum, Garden City, 87
Garden Peninsula Historical Society Museum, Garden, 147
Gardner House Museum, Albion, 39
Gaylord, 123
Gerald R. Ford Presidential Library, Ann Arbor, 67
Gerald R. Ford Presidential Museum, Grand Rapids, 19
Gilmore Car Museum, Hickory Corners, 22
Gladwin, 49
Gladwin County Historical Museum, Gladwin, 49
Gladwin County Historical Village, Gladwin, 49
Glawe School Museum, Rogers City, 134
Goodells, 87
Gordon Hall, Dexter, 81
Governor Warner Mansion, Farmington, 82
Grand Blanc, 88
Grand Blanc Heritage Association Museum, Grand Blanc, 88
Grand Haven, 18
Grand Ledge, 49
Grand Ledge Area Historical Society Museum, Grand Ledge, 49
Grand Marais, 147

Hellenic Museum of Michigan, Detroit, 80
Hemme Barn, Fraser, 86
Henry and Margaret Hoffman Annex, Rogers City, 134
Henry Ford Museum, Dearborn, 77
Heritage Hill Historic District, Grand Rapids, 19
Heritage House Farm Museum, Essexville, 47
Heritage Museum & Cultural Center, St. Joseph, 34
Heritage Museum, Menominee, 155
Heritage Room at the Richard L. Root Branch Library, Kentwood, 25
Heritage Village, Mackinaw City, 130
Hermansville, 149
Hessler Log Cabin, Old Mission, 132
Hickory Corners, 22
Hillman, 126
Hillsdale, 51
Hillsdale County Fairgrounds Museum, Hillsdale, 51
Historic Adventist Village, Battle Creek, 40
Historic Charlton Park Village and Museum, Hastings, 22
Historic Courthouse, Lapeer, 93
Historic Fishtown, Leland, 128
Historic Fort Wayne, Detroit, 80
Historic Mill Creek Discovery Park, Mackinaw City, 130
Historic Village at Goodells County Park, Goodells, 87
Historic Waterford Village, Waterford, 113
Historical Museum of Bay County, Bay City, 40
History Center (The Old Schoolhouse), Douglas, 16
History Center at Courthouse Square, Berrien Springs, 11
History Center of Traverse City, Traverse City, 136
Holland, 22
Holland Armory, Holland, 23
Holland Museum, Holland, 24
Holly, 91
Holocaust Memorial Center, Farmington HIlls, 83
Homer, 52
Honolulu House Museum, Marshall, 56
Houghton, 149
Houghton County Historical Museum, Lake Linden, 152
Houghton Lake, 127
Houghton Lake Area Historical Village, Houghton Lake, 127
Howell, 91
Howell Area Historical Society Museum, Howell, 91
Hubbardston, 52
Hubbardston Area Historical Society Museum, Hubbardston, 52
Huckleberry Railroad, Flint, 85
Hudson, 91
Hudson Museum, Hudson, 91
Huron County Historical Society, Bad Axe, 69
Huron Lightship, Port Huron, 102
Imlay City, 92

HELP US HELP PRESERVE MICHIGAN'S COLORFUL PAST

For more than 185 years, the Historical Society of Michigan—the oldest cultural organization in the state—has been committed to preserving our history. Isn't it time you joined in this effort? Here's a sampling of what your membership will support and what benefits you'll receive…

PUBLICATIONS

Every member receives HSM's quarterly magazine, the *Chronicle*. Upgrade to a higher level and you can get the award-winning magazine *Michigan History* and/or the respected academic journal *Michigan Historical Review*, too. You'll also earn discounts on HSM books, including the popular *Historic Michigan Travel Guide*.

CONFERENCES

As a member, you're eligible for discounted admission to HSM's annual State History Conference (fall) and the Upper Peninsula History Conference (summer), which combine tours, talks, and breakout sessions in an entertaining format. You can also join us for our annual Michigan in Perspective: The Local History Conference held each spring in the metro Detroit area.

EDUCATION

Are you a teacher? Enjoy discounts to our annual educator conference—Mulling Over Michigan—as well as lesson-plan supplements published in the *Chronicle*. HSM also coordinates the Michigan History Day (National History Day in Michigan) competition, which engages the historical and creative skills of 5,000 students each year.

AWARDS

Your membership fees also support an annual awards program that honors individual and organizational efforts to preserve Michigan history; recognition for historic family farms; and milestone plaques for businesses and organizations.

LOCAL SUPPORT

If you work with a local historical society, site, or museum, HSM provides you with special services that include calendar listings, promotional assistance, web hosting, training workshops, and more. Call (800) 692-1828 or visit www.hsmichigan.org/join for more information about organizational benefits.

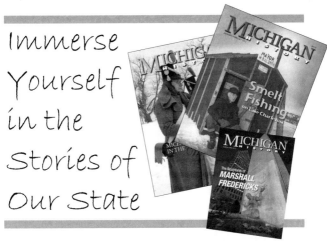

Immerse Yourself in the Stories of Our State

Michigan History is our state's popular-history publication. Edited for entertainment as much as education, it features stories of all kinds from Michigan's colorful past. Within its pages, you'll learn about logging, mining, manufacturing, and military history as well as art, architecture, music, sports, shipwrecks, and more.

Engaging Features
Among the valued features in every issue are "Remember the Time," a reader-written reminiscence; "Communiqués," a news section highlighting history happenings throughout the state; and "Conversations," an informative interview with a prominent professional working to preserve Michigan's history.

Informative Articles
A team of talented contributors generates the magazine's historical content—up to eight articles per issue. Samples of past-issue content may be found at *www.hsmichigan.org*.

Full-Color Graphics
Each issue is filled with colorful photographs, maps, and engravings collected from museums and archives around the state and the country. Besides being historically accurate, these images bring each story to life.

Timely Delivery
Michigan History is distributed six times a year, in February, April, June, August, October and December. As a subscriber, you'll receive the publication weeks before it's available on the newsstand.

Subscribe today by mailing us the following response form, visiting *www.hsmichigan.org/join,* **or calling (800) 366-3703!**

To become a member of the Historical Society of Michigan or subscribe to *Michigan History* magazine, complete this form and fax it to (517) 324-4370 or send it to the Historical Society of Michigan, 5815 Executive Drive, Lansing, MI 48911. For faster service, visit www.hsmichigan.org/join or call (800) 692-1828.

INDIVIDUAL HSM MEMBERSHIP

☐ Level 1 Membership - $25
    Includes *Chronicle*

☐ Level 2 Membership - $35
    Includes *Chronicle* and *Michigan Historical Review (MHR)*

☐ Level 3 Membership - $40
    Includes *Chronicle* and *Michigan History Magazine (MHM)*

☐ Level 4 Membership - $50
    Includes *Chronicle, MHR*, and *MHM*

ORGANIZATIONAL HSM MEMBERSHIP

For historical societies with a budget less than $25,000/year:

☐ Historical Society Membership - $35
    Includes *Chronicle* and *Michigan Historical Review (MHR)*

☐ Enhanced Historical Society Membership - $50
    Includes *Chronicle, Michigan History,* and *MHR*

For museums or libraries, or historical societies with a budget more than $25,000/year:

☐ Museum/Library Membership - $50
    Includes *Chronicle* and *Michigan Historical Review (MHR)*

☐ Enhanced Museum/Library Membership - $65
    Includes *Chronicle, Michigan History*, and *MHR*

MICHIGAN HISTORY MAGAZINE ONLY

☐ One-year *Michigan History* Subscription - $19.95
    HSM membership not included

☐ Two-year *Michigan History* Subscription - $34.95
    HSM membership not included

NAME_____

ADDRESS_____

CITY/STATE/ZIP_____

PHONE_____

E-MAIL (OPTIONAL)_____

PAYMENT

☐ Check payable to the Historical Society of Michigan
☐ Credit card: VISA, Discover, MasterCard, AMEX (see below)

CREDIT CARD NO._____

EXPIRATION DATE_____CVV_____

SIGNATURE_____

The Historical Society of Michigan

Founded in 1828 by Territorial Governor Lewis Cass and explorer Henry Schoolcraft, the Historical Society of Michigan (HSM) is the state's oldest cultural institution. The educational nonprofit focuses on five major mission areas: publications, conferences, education, awards and recognition programs, and support for local historical organizations.

Each year, the Society sponsors several conferences, including the State History Conference, Upper Peninsula History Conference, Michigan in Perspective (the Local History Conference), and Mulling Over Michigan.

.

The Society also publishes the quarterly magazine *Chronicle*, the bi-monthly *Michigan History* magazine, the *Historic Michigan Travel Guide,* and the *Michigan History Directory*. It also partners with Central Michigan University to distribute the academic journal *Michigan Historical Review* to HSM members with a Level 2 or Level 4 membership.

Its educational programs include Michigan History Day (National History Day in Michigan), educator training, workshops, and more. The Society also provides an array of support services, training, and outreach for the hundreds of local historical organizations in Michigan.

For more information, visit www.hsmichigan.org or call (517) 324-1828.

The Historical Society of Michigan
5815 Executive Drive
Lansing, MI 48911